YOU SHALL BE A
BLESSING

YOU SHALL BE A BLESSING

TWELVE LETTERS

ON THE

PRIESTHOOD

CARDINAL GERHARD MÜLLER

Translation by Susan Johnson

AVE MARIA PRESS AVE Notre Dame, Indiana

Gerhard Ludwig Müller, "Ihr sollt ein Segen sein". Zwöf Briefe über das Priestertum © 2018 Verlag Herder GmbH, Freiburg im Breisgau.

Websites used for English quotations:
New Advent, Fathers of the Church
The Catholic Encyclopedia

English edition © 2019 by Ave Maria Press, Inc.

Founded in 1865, Ave Maria Press is a ministry of the United States Province of Holy Cross.

www.avemariapress.com

Paperback: ISBN-13 978-1-59471-931-8

E-book: ISBN-13 978-1-59471-932-5

Cover photo of St. Peter and St. Paul by DeAgostini/Superstock.

Cover and text design by Samantha Watson.

Printed and bound in the United States of America.

Library of Congress Cataloging-in-Publication Data is available.

CONTENTS

Publisher's Note on Language

The word "man" with masculine pronouns is used throughout for *Mensch* but is to be understood inclusively as male and female individuals or humanity as a whole. This is done solely in order to avoid clumsy formulations or plurals where the individual is meant. Most Vatican documents and translations of older works also contain this usage.

PREFACE

With these letters on priestly ministry I wish to address myself to everyone who loves the Church of our Lord Jesus Christ. Only together can we fulfill the Church's universal mission for the salvation of all mankind. The good shepherd who gives his life for his sheep also sends the People of God pastors who accompany them on their pilgrimage of faith.

Before the resurrected Lord was raised into heaven to the Father, he gathered the eleven apostles and the other disciples, "led them out as far as Bethany, and, lifting up his hands, he blessed them" (Lk 24:50). It is the sacred ministry of the Church to bless all people with the fullness "of grace and truth" (cf. Jn 1:14). When the priests of Jesus Christ teach, lead, and sanctify the People of God, they are a blessing for the Church and all the whole. Jesus gave the apostles and their successors a share in his messianic power and mission (cf. *LG* 19; 28). With their "ministry and life" they praise "the God and Father of our Lord Jesus Christ, who has blessed us in Christ with every spiritual blessing in the heavenly places" (Eph 1:3).

For "by sacred ordination and mission which they receive from the bishops [priests] are promoted to the service of Christ the Teacher, Priest and King. They share in his ministry, a ministry whereby the Church here on earth is unceasingly built up into the People of God, the Body of Christ and the Temple of the Holy Spirit" (*PO* 1).

Everything is grounded in the historical self-communication of God, who "has spoken to us by a [or: the] Son" (Heb 1:2). And everything begins with the evangelist's historical testimony about the public ministry of Jesus, whom God himself had announced through the prophet as the one "who is to shepherd my people Israel" (Mt 2:6).

"Then Jesus went about all the cities and villages, *teaching* in their synagogues, and *proclaiming* the good news of the kingdom, and *curing* every disease and every sickness. When he saw the crowds, he had *compassion* for them, because they were harassed and helpless, like *sheep* without a *shepherd*" (Mt 9:35–36, italics mine). Then he said to his disciples, and thus to all believers in every age, "The harvest is plentiful, but the labourers are few; therefore ask the Lord of the harvest to send out labourers into his harvest" (Mt 9:37f.).

Dear Brothers and Sisters in Christ,

With the sacramental priesthood, the Sacrament of Matrimony, and the evangelical counsels, God gives his Church the gifts and charisms through which he wishes to build up his Church (cf. *LG* 11; 12). The theology and spirituality of the pastoral office of the priest concern all Christians because the Lord himself chooses people from out of the Church and appoints them as servants of grace and reconciliation. The shared care of all members of the Body of Christ for the salvation of all mankind reveals how fellow Christians each have their own vocations.

> In virtue of this catholicity each individual part contributes through its special gifts to the good of the other parts and of the whole Church. Through the common sharing of gifts and through the common effort to attain fullness in unity, the whole and each of the parts receive increase. Not only, then, is the People of God made up of different peoples but in its inner structure also it is composed of various ranks. This diversity among its members arises either by reason of their duties, as is the case with those who exercise the sacred ministry for the good of their brethren, or by reason of their condition and state of life, as is the case with those many who enter the religious state and, tending toward holiness

by a narrower path, stimulate their brethren by their
example. (*LG* 13)

So what follows is not about the professional ethics of priests,
which would only be of interest to the clergy. All are responsible
for all, and each for the whole. "Bear one another's burdens, and
in this way you will fulfill the law of Christ" (Gal 6:2). We all
share the responsibility for the seeds of religious vocations in the
Church to fall on good soil. Good Catholics suffer when priests
fail to live up to their calling and the credibility of the Church is
jeopardized. They should pray for good priests; but they should
also know what our faith teaches about this sacrament through
which servants of Christ are appointed for the Church.

Reverend Confreres and Aspirants,

I am pleased to comply with the frequently heard request to
commit to writing the thoughts I have expressed on our ministry
as priests during spiritual retreats and in theological papers. I
am choosing the literary genre of the letter for this because it
allows the personal and the factual to be more easily combined.
It is not just about the tasks we have to fulfill, but rather about
ourselves, whether we find human fulfillment in this ministry
and grow spiritually richer in God's love. This will also enable
a wider readership to participate in the discussion of a topic
that is crucial for the future of the Church and for each of us
personally.

Let us also remember the young people who sense a calling
to priestly ministry in their hearts. Let us pray for them, that
the Lord will show them the way he wants to walk with them.
Let us speak to them, have time for them. Let us accompany
them on their way with kindness and respect for their dignity
and freedom. Just as we all recognized our own vocations to the
priesthood through the mediation of convincing pastors, and
presumably not first and foremost through reading a book, we
should also be strengthened in our vocation through personal

words of encouragement from our confreres and from those of the faithful with whom we are associated spiritually and by bonds of friendship.

I wish to invite you, too, young friend, when you read these words, to take part in this dialogue. Perhaps Jesus' call to join in the work of building up his kingdom is already to be heard in your inner spiritual ear. The Church community you experience where you live ought to be the resonance chamber for Jesus' personal call to you. For the whole Church, the Christian families and communities are all jointly responsible for creating a climate in which religious vocations can grow.

> Parents and teachers and all who are engaged in any way in the education of boys and young men should so prepare them that they will recognize the solicitude of our Lord for his flock, will consider the needs of the Church, and will be prepared to respond generously when our Lord calls, saying, 'Here I am; send me!' (Is 6:8). This voice of the Lord calling, however, is never to be expected as something which in an extraordinary manner will be heard by the ears of the future priest. It is rather to be known and understood in the manner in which the will of God is daily made known to prudent Christians. These indications should be carefully noted by priests. *(PO* 11)

I myself look back with gratitude to my parents, teachers, and pastors, who did so much in my childhood and youth to make faith in Jesus Christ the unshakeable foundation upon which I stand. Taking my bearings from exemplary priests and faithful laity enabled the conviction to come to grow in me that I was called personally by Jesus Christ to priestly ministry.

So I wish to dedicate these letters on priesthood to a man who as a priest and religious studies teacher accompanied me spiritually and nurtured my theological thinking for the nine years in which I attended grammar school in Mainz: *Werner Krimm* (1928–2000). He died with a reputation for sanctity.

From Rome, on the fortieth anniversary of my priestly ordination,

11 February 2018
Cardinal Gerhard Müller

KEY ABBREVIATIONS

DOCUMENTS OF
THE SECOND VATICAN COUNCIL

AA   Decree on the Apostolate of the Laity (*Apostolicam Actuositatem*)

DV   Dogmatic Constitution on Divine Revelation (*Dei Verbum*)

GS   Pastoral Constitution on the Church in the Modern World (*Gaudium et Spes*)

LG   Dogmatic Constitution on the Church (*Lumen Gentium*)

OT   Decree on Priestly Training (*Optatam Totius*)

PO   Decree on the Ministry and Life of Priests (*Presbyterorum Ordinis*)

SC   Constitution on the Sacred Liturgy (*Sacrosanctum Concilium*)

TITLES OF WORKS
ARRANGED BY AUTHOR

Augustine
Civ.   *De civitate Dei*
Tr. in Io.   *Tractatus in Ioannem*

Bernard of Clairvaux
Ep.   *Epistula*

Hippolytus
TA   *Traditio Apostolica*

Ignatius of Antioch
IgnEph   *Epistula ad Ephesios*
IgnMag   *Epistula ad Magnesios*
IgnPhil   *Epistula ad Philadelphienses*
IgnRom   *Epistula ad Romanos*
IgnSym   *Epistula ad Smyrnaeos*
IgnTrall   *Epistula ad Trallianer*

Irenaeus of Lyon
Haer.   *Adversus haereses*

John Chrysostom
De sac.   *De sacerdotio*

Justin Martyr
Apol.   *Apologia*

Thomas Aquinas
S.th.   *Summa theologiae*
S.c.G.   *Summa contra gentiles*

GENERAL ABBREVIATIONS

CA   *Confessio Augustana*

Cat. Rom.   *Catechismus Romanus, seu Catechismus ex decreto Concilii Tridentini ad Parochos Pii Quinti Pont. Max. iussu editus,* ed. Pedro Rodriguez, Vatican City: Libreria Editrice Vaticana, 1989

CCC   *Catechism of the Catholic Church,* London: Geoffrey Chapman, 1994

Did.   *Didache*

DH   Denziger, Heinrich. *Enchiridion Symbolorum: Compendium of Creeds, Definitions, and Declarations on Matters of Faith and Morals (Latin–English)*, San Francisco: Ignatius Press, 2012

WA   Martin Luther, *Werke. Kritische Gesamtausgabe* (Weimarer Ausgabe)

1.

A THEOLOGY OF PRIESTHOOD FOR THE CORPORATE GOOD OF THE CHURCH

Dear Friends of the Catholic Faith,

I hope that as many Catholics as possible will be interested in these reflections on priesthood. What I am offering here is not, however, my own subjective opinions; no one called to priestly ministry could build his life on those. God alone is our foundation, and it is his word that we must listen to.

THE SOURCES FROM WHICH OUR FAITH SPRINGS

Theology is not about all the notions and different opinions about God. Instead, what it deals with is God's self-revelation in Jesus Christ, his Word, which became flesh (cf. Jn 1:14). It goes without saying that *sacred scripture* is not of merely historical importance for the theology of the priesthood. Rather, it represents the inexhaustible source from which the word of God flows like a river of living water, making the Church's soil fertile. The *apostolic tradition*, which is indissolubly linked to sacred scripture, "takes the word of God entrusted by Christ the Lord

1

and the Holy Spirit to the apostles, and hands it on to their successors in its full purity, so that led by the light of the Spirit of truth, they may in proclaiming it preserve this word of God faithfully, explain it, and make it more widely known" (*DV* 9).

The decisions of the popes and councils on questions of the doctrine and life of priests are not a norm imposed on us from outside. We Catholics understand the *magisterium* of the pope and of the bishops in communion with him as an authority that is a crucial component in the transmission of revelation. The Church's magisterium has been vested by the exalted Lord in the Holy Spirit with the gift of infallibility when teaching on questions of faith and morals.

The apostles and doctors of the Church have from the beginning right up to recent times provided the model for any spiritually fruitful theology and pastoral care.

The Church has been given wellsprings of theological and pastoral inspiration that will never run dry in immortal works by the Church Fathers on the pastoral office of priests. To begin with, there are the three pastoral letters of St. Paul to Timothy and Titus, which present and describe a prototype of the ministry and life of bishops and priests. Paul points the way equally clearly in the farewell speech he addresses to the "elders" of the church of Ephesus gathered in Miletus (cf. Acts 20:17–38). From among the classic writings on priesthood I would like to mention here only the Second Theological Oration of Gregory of Nazianzus, which he wrote in 362 in connection with his attempted flight from accepting priestly office. Alongside this are the famous six books by St. John Chrysostom "On the Priesthood" written in about AD 385. These have over and over again been a source of orientation for me. And to a certain extent they were what encouraged me to write the present letters, too. All this is great spiritual reading of the sort that should regularly accompany both seminarians as they prepare for their sacred vocation and priests in their spiritual exercises.

We priests, religious, and laity can find an introduction to the piety and reverence of the celebration of the sacrifice of the

Mass in St. Cyril's *Fifth Mystagogic Catechesis*, which is addressed to the newly baptized and was given in the Church of the Holy Sepulchre in Jerusalem in AD 348. Every year in the Daily Office for Weeks 24 and 25 we read St. Augustine's famous Sermon 46, *De pastoribus*. And who would not treasure St. Gregory the Great's *Regula pastoralis*, written in AD 591? Throughout the Middle Ages it served both priests and bishops as a mirror for their ministry. To this day, it provides the deep spirituality of a good shepherd after the image of the high priest Jesus Christ.[1]

A person may be able to quote all the relevant biblical passages, have studied the development of the official theology in the Church Fathers and Scholasticism, and know where to look up the decisions of the magisterium, but if that person does not hear the voice of Jesus saying to him personally, not to one of his neighbors: "Follow me. I am sending you," then he will remain a cold iron from which the spark of apostolic zeal for the house of God will never spring. But what we want is for people to be reminded when they see us at work, as they once were with Jesus, of the words of scripture:

Zeal for your house will consume me. (Jn 2:17)

FAITH COMES FROM HEARING AND IS REASONABLE

The Blessed Cardinal John Henry Newman (1801–1890) introduced existential needs into the somewhat abstract scholastic theology of his time. The motto on his coat of arms was: *Cor ad cor loquitur*. We do not believe in dogmas about the faith but rather in the living God who reveals himself to us in his Word (the Logos of God) and loves us in his Spirit. This does not contradict the Creed and the deep intellectual penetration of it in theology. There is, however, an irreversible sequence from *auditus fidei* to *intellectus fidei*. Faith comes from hearing the word of God (Rom 10:17), which we understand in the light of the Holy Spirit and accept in faith (*lumen fidei*), whereas theology is pursued with the light of natural reason as a science (*lumen naturale*). But it is reason illuminated by faith (*ratio fide illustrata*) that endows Christians with a rational and by no means blind faith and equips them with a reason that is not rationalistically restricted or a "weak reason" (*obsequium rationabile*).

COMMITTED TO THE HEAD OF THE CHURCH, JESUS CHRIST

Throughout the forty years of my ministry in the Church I have been moved over and over again by the words of the apostle in the light of the glory of Christ, who transforms us all into his own image (2 Cor 3:18). Paul says of himself and all the other apostles: "Therefore, since it is by God's mercy that we are engaged in this ministry, we do not lose heart. We have renounced the shameful things that one hides; we refuse to practise cunning or to falsify God's word; but by the open statement of the truth we commend ourselves to the conscience of everyone in the sight of God" (2 Cor 4:1f.).

When asked whether, after various experiences, some of them disappointing, I would offer myself for ordination again today, I reply with God's help and St. Paul as my model and witness: "I know the one in whom I have put my trust, and I am sure that he is able to guard until that day what I have entrusted to him" (2 Tim 1:12).

Putting up with the human limitations of one's superiors is often a hard test of faith. The same goes, the other way round, for others with respect to us, too. But at the center of my Creed stands Christ, who has gained the Church for himself as his "holy" bride (cf. Eph 5:27). When we examine our consciences, no one, from curate to cardinal, can escape the daily plea: "And forgive us our sins, for we ourselves forgive everyone indebted to us" (cf. Lk 11:4).

Ultimately it is not human beings but God alone that we have to answer to. The leaders of the Church, who "are keeping watch over" the faithful (as shepherds) (cf. Heb 13:17), will one day have to give account of their proclamation of the word of God, their faith, and the example they have set or failed to set to the faithful (cf. Heb 13:7, 17, 24). But "with fear and trembling" (Phil 2:12) as to my salvation, I do not give up hope that when the surely long list of my omissions is read out, I might in the end nevertheless hear the undeserved judgment: "[Y]ou have been trustworthy in a few things [. . .]; enter into the joy of your master" (Mt 25:23).

However, what most priests are seeking at this moment in the history of the world and the Church is not first and foremost theological *instruction* on the origins and essence, tasks and functions of the priesthood. What they sorely miss is spiritual *encouragement* amid all the stresses and strains of offering everyday pastoral care over vast parochial areas—even more so in face of the global denial of the possibility of knowing the truth and of its being necessary for one's salvation. None other than the Lord himself reassures us: "In the world you face persecution. But take courage; I have conquered the world!" (Jn 16:33).

It is therefore by no means a waste of time for us to reassure ourselves "carefully" (Lk 1:3)—as St. Luke does in his double work of gospel and Acts—of the foundations of our faith in Jesus Christ. This also goes analogously for our vocation, mission, and authorization for the salvific ministry that we as ordained priests exercise in the person of Christ, the head of the Church. For it is in his name that bishops and priests are to instruct the faithful with the word of God and sanctify them through the grace of his sacraments. To "sanctify" someone does not mean—along the lines of some cheap caricature of piety—alienating people from those around them and their work. The faithful are healed and sanctified through a true knowledge and love of God, which also includes loving one's neighbor and taking responsibility for the world, so as to do "good works, which God prepared beforehand to be our way of life" (Eph 2:10). As good shepherds they lead the People of God on their pilgrimage "amid the persecutions of the world and the consolations of God" (Augustine, *Civ.* 18,51,2) to eternal life. For, as successors of the apostles, priests should be thought of "as servants of Christ and stewards of God's mysteries" of whom it is required "that they should be found trustworthy" (1 Cor 4:1f.).

As a bishop and cardinal of the Roman Church, I would also like to stress today what the apostle Paul writes to Timothy, the prototype successor to the apostles. Let these words be commended to bishops, presbyters/priests, and all the faithful in the parishes:

> Let the elders (*presbyteroi*) who rule well be considered worthy of double honour, especially those who labour in preaching and teaching. (1 Tim 5:17)

First and foremost, I would like to offer encouragement to carry out your work in the Lord's vineyard quietly and calmly, with gratitude and joy. In a prayer that follows the Promise of the Elect and precedes the Litany of Supplication, the bishop ardently commends those called to priesthood to God's grace: "May God who has begun the good work in you bring it to fulfillment."

The Lord will not be sparing with praise for his faithful servant and the wise steward of his property. He rewards us by including us in his thanks to the Father. At every celebration of the Eucharist we give thanks in faith through, with, and in Jesus Christ for the "hope [that] does not disappoint us, because God's love has been poured into our hearts through the Holy Spirit that has been given to us" (Rom 5:5). "All priests, in union with bishops, [...] share in one and the same priesthood and ministry of Christ" (*PO* 7).

Therefore bishops should regard their priests as brothers and friends; and the latter should find in their bishop a paternal friend. For already since Patristic times, the bishop has been called *antonomastice sacerdos quasi summus sacerdos* (Thomas Aquinas, *Quodlibeta* III q.6 ad 1). The priests' material and especially their spiritual welfare should be a concern close to the bishop's heart, for "above all upon the bishops rests the heavy responsibility for the sanctity of their priests" (*PO* 7). In the communion of the priesthood, older priests should support their younger confreres with help and advice and by no means despise their youth (cf. 1 Tim 4:12).

As already mentioned, there is certainly no lack of learned studies on the biblical foundation and the dogmatic development of the Sacrament of Orders in the faith awareness of the Church. After all, we have a summary of magisterial statements on the "Ministry and Life of Priests" in the declarations of the Second Vatican Council. The decree *Presbyterorum Ordinis* (7.12.1965) must be read and expounded within the broad perspective of the Dogmatic Constitution on the Church (*Lumen Gentium*), especially of Chapter 3, "The Hierarchical Structure of the Church and in Particular the Episcopate" (21.11.1964). Unlike previous councils and papal doctrinal decisions, which had merely defended and defined individual constitutive elements of the Sacrament of Orders against errors, this constitution offers a positive and integrative overview. The synopsis of the most important magisterial statements on priesthood in Part II of the *Catechism of the Catholic Church* is also helpful: Section II deals with the seven sacraments of the Church.

At a time when the sacramental priesthood was being questioned most, the Council of Trent had defended the true and Catholic doctrine of the Sacrament of Orders in its *Decretum de sacramento ordinis* (15.07.1563). However, the Council Fathers confined themselves to defending the essential elements of the Catholic priesthood that were being called into question without presenting an overall positive and integral synthesis of the Church's teaching on the Sacrament of Orders.

The main topics were the institution of the priesthood by Christ, the various degrees of orders ranging from bishop, presbyter and (sub-)deacon to the minor orders, the sacramental nature of ordination and the resultant ecclesiastical hierarchy, along with the special powers of the priest with respect to the Sacrament of Penance and the offering of the eucharistic sacrifice. No less significant were the Council's resolutions on reform of the clerical office, especially its promotion of the residency requirement which distinguishes the good shepherd from the hireling. The good shepherd lives with his flock and accompanies it.

The *Decretum de reformatione* begins with a basic description of the nature and mission of priestly ministry: "Whereas it is by divine precept enjoined on all to whom the cure of souls is committed to know their own sheep; to offer sacrifice for them; and, by the preaching of the divine word, by the administration of the sacraments, and by the example of all good works, to feed them; to have a fatherly care of the poor and of other distressed persons, and to apply themselves to all other pastoral duties." Important, too, is the Roman Catechism (1566), which encapsulates the Council of Trent's ideal of the bishop and priest in the image of the good shepherd and indefatigable pastor.

Here we are in the midst of the sixteenth-century controversies with Martin Luther, Huldrych Zwingli, and Jean Calvin. The same topics continue to be relevant to reaching an ecumenical understanding on the nature and mission of the Church even today. This includes carefully determining the relationship between the universal or shared priesthood of all believers and the sacramental priesthood of the pastors of the Church.

STICKING TOGETHER IN TIMES OF CRISIS

I believe that it belongs to our service of the Church for us bishops, priests, and deacons to strengthen one another both spiritually and as human beings. This takes place through reflecting on the fundamentals of the Sacrament of Orders in the light of our experiences in our spiritual life and pastoral work. Modeling ourselves, as we all do, on Christ, the good shepherd of his sheep, the universal mediator of salvation, and the high priest of the new covenant, we, too, should share our hopes and cares like brothers. Yet we do not shun solitude, where the soul finds peace (*shalom*) and bliss (*beatitudo*) in God.

Isolation, however, is something quite different and nothing short of nihilistic despair. Here all of us are responsible for making sure that none of our confreres loses his faith in God, his optimism, and a healthy self-confidence. "How very good and pleasant it is when kindred live together in unity! [...] For there the Lord ordained his blessing, life for evermore" (Ps 133:1–3). By sharing in prayer and good conversation we protect ourselves against resignation and the travesty of its opposite, namely mindless routine. What wears us down even more is the cynicism that arises from tedium and disappointment, which can easily turn into a contempt for the faithful and weariness of the Church. The temptation to give up on oneself spiritually and intellectually rises up from the abyss of doubting God's faithfulness. It devours the holy zeal with which we began the good work (cf. Phil 1:6).

But the words of the Lord hold true: "The rain fell, the floods came, and the winds blew and beat on that house, but it did not fall, because it had been founded on rock" (Mt 7:25). Let us pray over and over again in times of doubt, when we feel abandoned by God and man: "Blessed be the Lord, my rock" (Ps 144:1).

The rock upon which our priesthood stands is Jesus Christ. He is not just some prophet or other, much less a false Messiah. Jesus of Nazareth, "the son of Mary" (Mk 6:3), is "Jesus Christ, the Son of God" (Mk 1:1). The message that the "angel of the Lord" (Lk 2:9) proclaimed to the shepherds in the fields outside Bethlehem is also addressed to us today, the pastors of Christ's Church. As "angels of the Church" (cf. Rev 2:1), we are to proclaim the gospel of Christ to all people: "Do not be afraid; for see—I am bringing you good news of great joy for all the people: to you is born this day in the city of David a *Saviour*, who is the *Messiah*, the *Lord*" (Lk 2:10f, italics mine).

The priest "who *hears* these words of mine and *acts* on them will be like a wise man who built his house on rock" (Mt 7:24, italics mine) and not on sand. And this rock is Christ (cf. 1 Cor 10:4).

Just as the Israelites survived in the wilderness because "all ate the same spiritual food, and all drank the same spiritual drink" (1 Cor 10:3f.), the new People of God lives through the God-Man Jesus Christ.

> I am the living bread that came down from heaven. Whoever eats of this bread will live for ever; and the bread that I will give for the life of the world is my flesh. [. . .] Those who eat my flesh and drink my blood have eternal life, and I will raise them up on the last day; for my flesh is true food and my blood is true drink. Those who eat my flesh and drink my blood abide in me, and I in them. Just as the living Father sent me, and I live because of the Father, so whoever eats me will live because of me. (Jn 6:51–57)

If the Son of God continues his mission in his apostles, the priest for his part lives from daily communion with Christ in the eucharistic sacrifice. Let us ask for perseverance and constancy that we might one day say with the apostle: "I have fought the good fight, I have finished the race, I have kept the faith" (2 Tim 4:7). In those hours when we doubt our vocation—and that even happened to some of the disciples on seeing the risen Jesus (cf. Mt 28:17)—the words of the apostle in 2 Corinthians 6:1–10 will be a comfort to us, especially v. 10: we are "in pain yet always full of joy; poor and yet making many people rich; having nothing, and yet owning everything" (NJB).

IT IS HIGH TIME
TO ENCOURAGE PRIESTS

Priests deserve clear words of encouragement from the superior and supreme ecclesiastical authorities. One would like to shout out to them the words of the apostle: "Fathers, do not provoke your children, or they may lose heart" (Col 3:21). For "on account of this communion in the same priesthood and ministry, bishops should regard priests as their brothers and friends" (*PO* 7). By means of bad experiences with the visible Church, God wishes to teach us not to rely on human beings but only on his faithfulness towards us. The lessons with which God teaches his servants are bound to be painful for us. But that does not justify an authoritarian leadership style. Like Paul, I find myself asking: "Am I now seeking human approval, or God's approval?" (Gal 1:10). And the apostle concludes as far as he himself is concerned: "If I were still pleasing people, I would not be a servant of Christ" (Gal 1:10). It is not either primarily or ultimately our own sensitivities that matter but rather that a door is opened for the word of God. What counts is that "as servants of God we have commended ourselves in every way" (2 Cor 6:4).

Let us bishops take as our model St. Paul, who calls his coworker Timothy "my loyal child in the faith" (1 Tim 1:2), "my beloved child" (2 Tim 1:2), and addresses Titus as "my loyal child in the faith we share" (Ti 1:4). He encourages Timothy by talking about his own calling: "I am grateful to Christ Jesus our Lord, who has strengthened me, because he judged me faithful and appointed me to his service" (1 Tim 1:12). And he urges him to "fight the good fight, having faith and a good conscience" (1 Tim 1:18f.) and to "be a good servant of Christ Jesus, nourished on the words of the faith and of the sound teaching that you have followed" (1 Tim 4:6).

At the Last Supper Jesus revealed the true meaning of higher authority in the Church. Only if we commend ourselves to the Lord, who prays for us that our faith may not fail, can we fufill his commission to "strengthen your brothers" (Lk 22:32). What "Paul, Silvanus, and Timothy" (1 Thess 1:1) write "as apostles of Christ" (1 Thess 2:7) to the church of Thessalonia should apply by analogy to the relationship of religious superiors, bishops, and the pope to the priests: "You are witnesses, and God also, how pure, upright, and blameless our conduct was towards you believers. As you know, we dealt with each one of you like a father with his children, urging and encouraging you and pleading that you should lead a life worthy of God, who calls you into his own kingdom and glory" (1 Thess 2:10–12). We bishops should bear in mind that the "authority, which the Lord gave [is] for building you up and not for tearing you down" (2 Cor 10:8).

What harm has been caused over the course of Church history by the willful, selfish use of ecclesiastical authority? A considerable amount of anticlericalism has resulted from the blinkered and vain abuse of ecclesial power. People imagined they were serving God when they humiliated the novices and ordinands entrusted to their care in order to teach them humility. "Breaking their will" was thought to be the royal road to the virtue of obedience. But virtues come from inside through grace. They cannot be forced from outside. Priority must be given to serving, not ruling. A wise spiritual director exercises restraint because he knows that there is only *one* teacher and that we are all pupils and each other's brothers. Jesus did after all say: "All who exalt themselves will be humbled, and all who humble themselves will be exalted" (Mt 23:12).

Take, for example, the case of the French Curé Jean Meslier (1664–1729), a hero of free thinkers and atheists. Up to his death, he outwardly performed all his pastoral duties faithfully. His justified protests against the maltreatment of the peasants by their overlords were not well received by his archbishop. This exalted gentleman was closer to the lived reality of feudal society than to God's unseasonable justice on the side of the poor. The curé was subjected to a process of public humiliation by his archbishop. It was from the lifelong wound this left in the disenchanted man that flowed his posthumously published memoirs, which were full of hatred and resentment and came to have a great impact on the anti-Church wing of the Enlightenment. When love turns into disappointment, clerical apostates become not only the worst critics of the Church but also enemies of God. Our clandestine author sought to debunk all religions as "of human invention, and full of errors and deceptions." In the French Revolution, and later in the bloodiest persecutions of the Church, this was to justify the "heroic acts" of liberating mankind from brainwashing, superstition, and clerical power. Now no matter what we do and say, it is always suspected of being ideology. People think that however selflessly a cleric might act, in reality this is not done for the sake of truth and salvation but rather to serve his own interests. And once the credibility of the Church has been shattered by the misconduct of bishops and priests, it is hard to restore. The priest is an image of Christ and a model for the faithful. Hence his responsibility is all the greater.

OFFICE AND PERSON:
A SALUTARY DISTINCTION

We do well to recall once more the ancient and well-founded distinction between office and person that entered clearly into the faith awareness of the Church during the Donatist Controversy.

For subordinates this distinction is a consolation since it means that they do not have to despair of Christ and the Church on account of the inadequacies of their all-too-human representatives. For superiors it is a warning not to hide their intellectual and character weaknesses behind the authority of Christ and the Church. Just think of the contempt and ingratitude with which Henri de Lubac, S.J. (1896–1991), one of the truly great theologians of Vatican II who had, however, once been suspected of modernism, was treated by his superiors in the Society of Jesus at the end of his days simply because he no longer fitted into their "progressive" mold. Ingratitude and ostracism are the fruit of the kind of thinking in stereotypes that ideological delusion brings with it.

The greatest abuse of ecclesiastical office results from confusing spiritual authority with temporal power. Every officeholder in the Church, from religious superior to bishop, becomes a source of harm to the Church and to his pastoral care if he uses his spiritual authority as an opportunity to impose his private notions and subjective grievances on the brothers entrusted to his care or on the whole Church. Even in the nurturing of vocations, the priestly ideal put together by the pastoral department of a diocese or religious order with borrowings from psychology and sociology cannot be elevated to the status of being ultimately the crucial criterion. People seek priests after the heart of Jesus, who "gave himself up for her [the Church], in order to make her holy by cleansing her with the washing of water by the word" (Eph 5:25f.).

In the public perception, scandals concerning priests are generally laid at the door of the Church and thus damage her credibility. But the Church's credibility is the portal to salvific faith. Consequently, serious moral misconduct on the part of priests constitutes a violation of the sanctity of the sacraments and the Church, the Body of Christ, of whose head they are visible representations, not merely an offense under the civil code. "Priests are made in the likeness of Christ the Priest by the Sacrament of Orders, so that they may, in collaboration with their bishops, work for the building up and care of the Church which is the whole Body of Christ, acting as ministers of him who is the Head" (*PO* 12). On account of hirelings in clerical clothes, even good and diligent priests as a group—deemed guilty by association—are welcome victims for anticlerical prejudice and media-orchestrated money making. Here it is absolutely essential to distinguish clearly between the sort of transgressions and weaknesses that scarcely any Christian can completely avoid on his or her pilgrimage through life and intentionally leading a moral double life.

The priest as pastor of the parish should be a model (*typos, forma gregis*) for his flock since he represents the "chief shepherd," *princeps pastorum* (1 Pt 5:4), Christ, "the shepherd and guardian of your souls" (1 Pt 2:25). "Be imitators of me, as I am of Christ" (1 Cor 11:1), Paul writes to his Corinthians. Timothy is to be "an example to those who would come to believe in him for eternal life" (1 Tim 1:16). Paul urges his star pupil to "set the believers an example (*typos*) in speech and conduct, in love, in faith, in purity" (1 Tim 4:12). Hence the gross misconduct of priests is doubly serious as it compromises preaching and severely tests the faith of the weaker (cf. John Chrysostom, *De sac.* VI, 12). That is why strict criteria must apply to the selection of future priests. The candidates must themselves also undertake an extremely conscientious self-examination (cf. John Chrysostom, *De sac.* III, 10). An unworthy or bad shepherd destroys the People of God (cf. Ezek 34). If it can be said of priests of the Old Covenant that they have "made the house of Israel stumble into iniquity" (Ezek 44:12; cf. Hos 5:1; 9:8), this is even more the case with priests of Christ and his Church: "For certainly no one does more harm in the Church than one who has the name and rank of sanctity, while he acts perversely" (Gregory the Great, *Regula pastoralis* I, 2).

"A priest who has vowed chastity" (Thomas Aquinas, *S.th.* I-II q.73 a.10) will have the sin counted against him more as guilt because of the bad example it sets, his lack of gratitude for the high dignity he has received, and the contradiction between his sinful deed and his sacramental representation of Christ.

For this reason, alongside seeking perfection "as your heavenly Father is perfect" (Mt 5:48), ordination obliges the priest "to acquire that perfection in special fashion" (*PO* 12). Since "every priest in his own fashion acts in place of Christ himself, he is enriched by a special grace, so that, as he serves the flock committed to him and the entire People of God, he may the better grow in the grace of him whose tasks he performs, because to the weakness of our flesh there is brought the holiness of him who for us was made a High Priest 'holy, guiltless, undefiled, not reckoned among us sinners' (Heb 7:26)" (*PO* 12).

2.

PRIESTS AFTER
THE HEART OF JESUS

Dear Confreres and Fellow Christians,

The Church needs bishops and priests after the heart of Jesus, not after the mind of man. In the Bible, "heart" stands for commitment to others and not for sentimentality with oneself. A good pastor loves people because he loves them in Christ; he does not make himself popular with them because he loves himself in them.

The heart of Jesus, which was pierced by the soldier's lance on the Cross, is the open heart of the good shepherd who gives his life for his sheep. Hence we can only be priests of Christ if our hearts are open in love for his sheep.

The Second Vatican Council not only pointed out on more than one occasion the "excellence of the order of priests in the Church" but also spoke of "tasks of the greatest importance and of ever increasing difficulty" being given to this order "in the renewal of Christ's Church" (*PO* 1). Without priests there is no new evangelization and no overcoming of the "crisis of man without God." As a servant of Christ and custodian of God's mysteries, the priest bears witness in his words and life to the openness of the human spirit to transcendence. For in his or her spiritual and physical existence every human being is referenced to God as the origin, meaning, and goal of the whole of creation.

The origin and meaning of priesthood lie in the commissioning of men to serve Christ for mankind. We are chosen from among mortals by Christ, the high priest of the new covenant, and "put in charge of things pertaining to God on their behalf" (Heb 5:1). Corresponding to our right to dogmatic truth and moral clarity is the duty of both pope and bishops "to strengthen your brothers" (Lk 22:32) and avoid any confusion.

When the dogmatic rug is pulled from under the feet of the priesthood, the ethics and spirituality of this ministry hang in the air. Here, in the usage of Catholic theology, the word "dogmatic" does not refer to human theories about God but rather to the facts of revelation and salvation history as they are known to us from the word of God and presented by the magisterium as articles of faith. The dogmatic foundation of the "ministry and life of priests" is the fact of the apostolate's being instituted by Jesus Christ and tangibly continued in the mission and powers of bishop, presbyters, and deacons.

Jesus first called the twelve apostles, with Simon Peter at their head, and then the seventy-two disciples into a community of responsibility for his Church. They form a corporate body with a head and many members which continues in the College of Bishops. Thus, the constitution of the Church already shows itself in principle to be a *communio ecclesiarum* with Rome, the *ecclesia principalis*. The Roman Church is the visible head, mother, and teacher of the *Catholica*. This basic principle can also be seen in the unity of the bishop with his presbyters. "Jesus Christ, the Son of God" (Mk 1:1) did not want to send his messengers out singly, isolated and having to shift for themselves; rather, he "sent them on ahead of him *in pairs* to every town and place where he himself intended to go" (Lk 10:1, italics mine).

So we are ambassadors of Jesus Christ, who "is truly the Saviour of the world" (Jn 4:42). On our shoulders lies nothing less than jointly looking after "the salvation of your souls" (1 Pt 1:9). This is not something arbitrary and interchangeable; it is all-or-nothing, a matter of every individual's being or nonbeing before God in time and eternity.

Christ has called priests "to tend the flock of God" (1 Pt 5:2). Hence they can say to the faithful: we are sent to you in the name and with the authority of Christ, "the shepherd and guardian of your souls" (1 Pt 2:25; cf. 5:2f.). We do not have earthly interests in mind. We are not after your money. We do not play power games. Rather, "by the open statement of the truth we commend ourselves to the conscience of everyone in the sight of God" (2 Cor 4:2). Our message is "the gospel of the glory of Christ, who is the image of God" (2 Cor 4:4).

And now follows the key phrase of priestly spirituality, words that stir the spirit, the soul, and the heart of the good shepherd day by day:

> For we do not proclaim ourselves; we proclaim Jesus Christ as Lord and ourselves as your slaves for Jesus' sake. (2 Cor 4:5)

Every priest today should apply to himself personally Paul's words to Timothy, his "beloved child" (1 Tim 1:2), and his coworkers, reminding them:

> to rekindle the gift of God that is within you through the laying on of my hands. (2 Tim 1:6)

When you, dear confrere, *are* purely and simply *there for* "those who believe and know the truth" (1 Tim 4:3), then "you will be a good servant of Christ Jesus, nourished on the words of the faith and of the sound teaching that you have followed" (1 Tim 4:6).

How can I be a "servant of Christ and steward of God's mysteries" (cf. 1 Cor 4:1) right from the start, and how can I become so more and more in my life?

A Great Task or Superhuman Burden?

Is it not hubris to want to be a servant of God? Are we not totally out of our depth when we appear in the temple and house (*oikos*) of the Lord as stewards (*oikonomoi*) of his mysteries, that is, the word and grace of God?

On the other hand, it is true that "whoever aspires to the office of bishop desires a noble task" (1 Tim 3:1). The risen Lord gave his disciples the promise that he would fill every priestly vocation with spirit and life: "But you will receive power when the Holy Spirit has come upon you; and you will be my witnesses in Jerusalem, in all Judea and Samaria, and to the ends of the earth" (Acts 1:8).

All the same, we are merely the stewards and dispensers of God's salvific mysteries (*dispensatores mysteriorum*) (1 Cor 4:1 Vulg.), not the originators of grace. Grace emanates solely from Christ, the head of the Church, and is passed on to his Body. That is why the efficacy of a priest's action depends on the powers conferred on him by Christ, not on his personal holiness and human authority. The ministers of the Church are not mediators of grace but rather stewards of the sacraments of grace—*ministris ecclesiae non est dare gratiam, sed gratiae sacramenta* (Thomas Aquinas, *S.th.* q.36 a.3).

The nagging doubt in our hearts can be overcome in the Spirit of God. With renewed apostolic zeal, we respond with an existential and not merely intellectual reply to the question raised by the history of philosophy: Has the Catholic Church—despite all the great renewal movements—not in fact been in an inexorable state of retreat since the Enlightenment and the upheavals of the French Revolution, a retreat that will one day end in a situation in which Christians will make up only a tiny minority of society?

But hidden in this question is the misunderstanding that the quantitative proportion of Christians and their cultural influence in society constitute the criteria for the truth and viability of their faith. The context of Jesus' question: "when the Son of Man comes, will he find faith on earth?" already reveals the answer: "And will not God grant justice to his chosen ones who cry to him day and night?" (Lk 18:7f.).

Yes, we are sometimes tired and feel like giving up. "Let others see to it that the faith and the Church continue!" Isn't that what an inner voice whispers to us? Don't we have the feeling, like Elijah, of being the only ones left "for the Israelites have forsaken your covenant" (1 Kgs 19:10)? We would like nothing better than to lie down like the prophet under a broom tree and call to God: "It is enough; now, O Lord, take away my life, for I am no better than my ancestors" (1 Kgs 19:4).

GOD'S STEADFAST FAITHFULNESS

But God does not abandon his prophets. Just as he sent an angel from heaven to his Son when he was in mortal anguish on the Mount of Olives to give him strength (cf. Lk 22:43), so the angel will touch your shoulder, too, and say to you, his prophet: "Get up and eat, otherwise the journey will be too much for you [. . .] to Horeb the mount of God" (1 Kgs 19:7f.).

In the Most Holy Eucharist, which we priests celebrate in the name of Jesus for and with the whole Church, it is not an angel that strengthens us. The Son of God himself, who took on our flesh and blood, offers us the food and drink to give us strength for our pilgrimage "to Mount Zion and to the city of the living God, the heavenly Jerusalem, [. . .] and to the spirits of the righteous made perfect, and to Jesus, the mediator of a new covenant" (Heb 12:22–24).

The Church is Christ's flock, and the pilgrim People of God are on their way to the heavenly Jerusalem. When the faithful feel their shepherds' readiness to make sacrifices as guardians of their souls (cf. 1 Pt 2:25), they should recognize in us the Spirit and strength of Jesus, the shepherd of shepherds and all of his sheep. And they will call to mind the word of scripture: "Zeal for your house will consume me" (Jn 2:17; cf. Ps 69:9).

But the shepherd is not without his flock. The priest and the faithful share a mutual responsibility. So let the community be reminded with "all your leaders and all the saints" (Heb 13:24) of the apostle's words: "Remember your leaders, those who spoke the word of God to you; consider the outcome of their way of life, and imitate their faith" (Heb 13:7) and then: "Obey your leaders and submit to them, for they are keeping watch [like shepherds] over your souls and will give an account. Let them do this with joy and not with sighing—for that would be harmful to you" (Heb 13:17; cf. *1 Clem* 1,3).

3.

PRIESTS OF THE LOGOS: WITNESSES TO THE MEANING OF HUMAN EXISTENCE

Dear Confreres and Fellow Christians,

So I by no means see it as a waste of time nor presumptuous to tackle the questions and doubts about the meaning of your priesthood that arise in a world in which quite a few people live their lives "as if God did not exist." Such people regard us as tragicomic figures that you do not know whether to laugh or cry about. And it is not pleasant to be eyed with surreptitious grins as a relic from a bygone world. After all, who wants to assume the role of the sad clown in public opinion? Any ignoramus can irritate us with scandals from the Church's history, even if all he can do is just repeat a few catchphrases about them. Do we not feel the same way as the apostles when they were faced with the glittering paganism of the ancient world, which regarded the message of the Cross as some foolishness from the Orient (cf. 1 Cor 1:23)? That "we have become a spectacle to the world, to angels and to mortals. We are fools for the sake of Christ" (1 Cor 4:9f.)? They stare at us with looks of irony and sarcasm like those that the "leaders of the people with their soldiers" cast at Jesus on the Cross. They "scoffed" and provoked our Lord Jesus, and their Redeemer, too, with the words: "He saved others; let him save himself if he is the Messiah of God, his chosen one!" (Lk 23:35). Where now is the power of the Church in the modern or postmodern era? Or, to paraphrase Ioseb Jughashvili alias Stalin: "How many divisions does the Pope have?"

I share your and all our worries about the Church, which is prostrating itself before secularism, preferring to secularize itself rather than pointing the world to the "wholly other" (Karl Barth), to God, its liberator and Savior. Priesthood is not a job that you take on or give up according to the principle of "supply and demand." If all we wanted was to mourn bygone days or jump on the bandwagon of the *zeitgeist*, we would be like Don Quixote, the "Knight of the Woeful Countenance."

You cannot leave God's service, for God has laid his hand upon you. The apostle is aware of the drama of his calling when he himself warns: "woe betide me if I do not proclaim the gospel! For if I do this of my own will, I have a reward; but if not of my own will, I am entrusted with a commission. What then is my reward? Just this: that in my proclamation I may make the gospel free of charge, so as not to make full use of my rights in the gospel" (1 Cor 9:16–18).

This is not about the economy of money and goods; rather, it refers to the economy of grace and truth. For "From his fullness we have all received, grace upon grace" (Jn 1:16). Nor is it about the exchange of commodities and material goods between needy people. Paul speaks of the *oikonomia salutis*, the accomplishment of God's plan for salvation, a "holy exchange." "For you know the generous act of our Lord Jesus Christ, that though he was rich [i.e., in his divinity], yet for your sakes he became poor [i.e., he became human], so that by his poverty you might become rich" (2 Cor 8:9).

God is the sole and greatest entrepreneur of all times and eternities, who invests everything in his "enterprise," the creation of the world and mankind, and never takes anything out of it. That is what is unparalleled in the relationship between God and us human beings. He does not live from us; we live from him. The Triune God does not give us human beings life and existence in order to make up for the deficit of his loneliness. He does not need us because he in any way requires human praise in order to increase his sense of self-worth.

SUSTAINED BY GOD'S GOODNESS

God is essentially and eternally just infinite goodness and love. He lacks nothing. By willing his own goodness, in the act of creation he wills that finite being exists and does so as participation in his goodness. The vast multitude of people who have existed over the course of world history, the inexhaustible richness of the coming into being of all forms of life, and the constellations of material things are the manifestation of the infinite goodness that he is in his divine nature from all eternity (cf. Thomas Aquinas, *S.c.G.* I, q.81).

Let it just be mentioned in passing that the fact and teaching of biological evolution only seemingly support atheism. The denial of the existence of God constitutes no more than the correct conclusion from the false premises of a metaphysical and epistemological materialism. If, however, creation is understood as participation in the being through which things exist in their natures and individualities, then the findings of the modern natural sciences and their technical applications are coherent with the philosophical conviction of the existence of God. With the natural light of reason we are capable of knowing him as the originator of all contingent being. In philosophical reflection we can arrive at the well-founded conviction of the creation of the universe out of the goodness of God. God is the origin and the goal of everything that exists besides him and is moving towards the goal of its own perfection.

The logic of love goes infinitely far beyond providing practically for life, the rules of the market and the exchange of commodities between beings with needs. Love "does not insist on its own way" (1 Cor 13:5). Love is generous and unstinting. It is not calculating but only has the well-being and salvation of the other in mind. For "God is love, and those who abide in love

abide in God, and God abides in them" (1 Jn 4:16). So who can
then harden his heart in unbelief and persist in doubt when he
learns the truth that the disciples profess?

> For God so loved the world that he gave his only Son,
> so that everyone who believes in him may not perish
> but may have eternal life. (Jn 3:16)

How can we bishops and priests serve the economy of divine
salvation as successors to the apostles with such conviction and
so convincingly as to be acceptable to God, "who desires everyone to be saved and to come to the knowledge of the truth. For
there is one God; there is also one mediator between God and
humankind, Christ Jesus, himself human" (1 Tim 2:4–5)?

   This is the question upon which everything revolves here.
After all, we are "servants of Christ and stewards of God's mysteries" (1 Cor 4:1), of word and sacrament in the house of God.
Priests should see themselves as "fishers of people" (Mk 1:17,
NJB) and say with the apostle: "Therefore, knowing the fear of
the Lord, we try to persuade others" (2 Cor 5:11), that is, win
them for Christ.

   The priestly office is a sacred calling and a divine vocation,
which demands our whole being and life and decides whether
we ultimately succeed or fail (cf. 1 Cor 4:4f.). "[A]nd woe betide
me if I do not proclaim the gospel!" (1 Cor 9:16), the apostle to
the Gentiles tells himself—and us.

Stay at Your Post Even with a Headwind or No Wind at All

In the days of sailing ships, people learned the art of tacking
against the wind. You can make progress and arrive at your des-
tination even against the wind. What was even more dangerous
on the ocean than a headwind was being becalmed. The same
is true of pastoral care. If the lack of interest is so great that no

one even contradicts us any more, all we can do is pray: "God is able from these stones to raise up children to Abraham" (Lk 3:8).

But we, too, are frail human beings who would prefer to be borne along gently on the waves of the mainstream than to constantly feel the icy wind of indifference and rejection blowing in our faces. We certainly want to work hard. But why should I forgo the comforts of a secure bourgeois life?—so the tempter inside us asks.

The maxim "in season and out of season" (2 Tim 4:2) runs lightly off the tongue. But it has often been easier to continue to proclaim sound doctrine undeterred in the face of threats than in the face of the sweet venom of flattery. "You're really too good for the priesthood. With your good looks you could easily find a good-looking wife, and you'd be a good father. With your gifts you could make a quite different career for yourself somewhere other than in the Church. The social prestige of priests has hit rock bottom after the abuse scandals—and you want to join that club?" This is the sort of thing priests often hear while they are still young. When you get older, people start pitying you as a hopeless case because you have not "enjoyed" your life and now "you've missed the boat."

But it is not only the individual challenges we face in preaching and pastoral care that cast doubt on the meaning of the priest's vocation and lifestyle; there is also the general cultural climate with its shifting intellectual paradigms and attitudes to life which change from one generation to the next. In view of the domination of positivism in science; monist materialism in the way the world and mankind are viewed; and relativism in philosophy, religion, and morals, it is hard to find either a starting point for the theocentricity of revealed religion and the radical Christ-centeredness of Church life or a way into the thoughts and feelings of many of our contemporaries.

There still remains a vague feeling that "man does not live by bread alone," but people do not dare to yield to the longing for "every word that comes from the mouth of God" (Mt 4:4) in their own lives. If—in the words of nineteenth-century criticism

of religion—there is no God, and if therefore hope in his work
of redemption were to prove illusory, then the Church could
not be "in Christ like a sacrament or as a sign and instrument
both of a very closely knit union with God and of the unity of
the whole human race" (*LG* 1).

Given these agnostic premises and their consequences for
man's self-understanding, "modernity" and "postmodernity"
present themselves as an overcoming of man's orientation
towards God, which is rejected as a false and hence outdated
consciousness stemming from "pre-modern" and "medieval"
thinking. Here "modernity" and "medieval" are not descriptions
of historical epochs but are used rather as normative categories
that determine the truth of the collective consciousness. If with
the beginning of the "Modern Age" or the "Enlightenment" a
paradigm shift took place in which the basic insights of an overall vision of reality founded on divine self-revelation no longer
appeared self-evident, then this seemingly cuts the ground from
under the Church as the "universal sacrament of salvation" (*LG*
48) in Christ and the sacramental priesthood.

People today fondly believe themselves to be enlightened
about the interest-determined nature of the Church's claims to
truth and power. They react to her representatives with embar-
rassment, disconcertment, scorn, and hatred. Almost inevitably,
a young man's decision to follow Jesus' call to serve as a priest
will meet with incomprehension and rejection, even in his own
family. He comes under suspicion of being naïve or of con-
sciously or unconsciously striving for power, prestige, or material advantage. Who has not then recalled Jesus' words: "and
you will be hated by all because of my name. But the one who
endures to the end will be saved" (Mk 13:13)?

In the conflict between loyalty to their inherited faith and
wanting to be up-to-date, many of the faithful today and quite
a few priests, too, get the impression of clinging to an illusion-
ary ideal that has been overtaken by modernity. And now, they
think, we have to throw out the ballast of obsolete doctrines on
faith and morals in order to justify ourselves to the dominant

ideologies as being compatible with them. A Christianity without dogma and sacraments does not go down well, so let's have a try at counselling and social utopia—that's the idea of our brave "reformers," who want to "rethink" everything, and yet just end up with the old heresies. Where the right of Christianity and the religious liberty of the citizens to exist at all is not radically disputed, even with bloodshed—as was the case in the culture wars and struggles between Church and state of the nineteenth century—what the Church is offered if she abandons her revealed faith is a niche in which to seek a utilitarian justification of herself as a "civil religion"[2] or a secular rational religion.[3] For the ideologically neutral state, they argue, needs a common basis of ethical and cultural values, and for that the Church should provide a spiritual space for mastering contingency or should make herself useful as a humanistic, charitable NGO.

The priest as "a servant of Jesus Christ, called to be an apostle, set apart for the gospel of God" (Rom 1:1) mutates into a functionary and propagandist of a system of socio-spiritual offers. He can now "sell" himself—unfortunately in the saddest meaning of the word—better as a provider of spiritual services at turning points in people's lives and at family celebrations.

An existence of this kind, abandoned by the Spirit, which in place of the healing truth of Christ offers people merely a placebo that deadens the nihilism, is not something anyone would aspire to. When I do not hold Christ's message to be true, why then should I risk my life for him? Every Christian, and first and foremost every priest, must keep focused on the truth and reality of God's revelation and salvific action in his Son: "If for this life only we have hoped in Christ, we are of all people most to be pitied. But in fact Christ has been raised from the dead, the first fruits of those who have died" (1 Cor 15:19–20).

The witnesses and messengers of this truth are the apostles and their successors in the office of bishop and priest.

AGAINST THE IMMANENTIST SHORTENING OF HORIZONS

Whereas in several continents belief in Jesus the Savior of all mankind is spreading and taking root in their cultures, there is a neo-pagan fury raging in those countries with a longstanding Christian tradition. This neo-paganism is obsessed with the idea that people will be liberated and made happy by ripping hope in the living God out of their hearts.

Religion, they contend, is opium for the masses, helping people forget their wretchedness and sapping their revolutionary energy to save themselves. Instead of allowing oneself to be constrained by the laws of the Creator, what is now called for, so they claim, is to venture boldly on recreating humanity. Whatever key criticism of religion is played in, the fundamental tone always remains the same: man has given up this life, which is after all his only existence, for the sake of an imaginary afterlife. Under the pretext of liberating people from alienation through the Christian faith and enabling them to determine their own happiness themselves, whole armies of enlightened intellectuals, pedagogues, propagandists, and political agitators have been slaving away for 300 years in governments and parliaments, in the media and writing to the papers, in order to eradicate the last vestiges of a Christian concept of mankind. Faced with the threats of those waging the cultural war and seduced by the sweet-sounding claims of those who claim to be the liberators of the people from the Church's tutelage, quite a number of people have in fact allowed themselves to be lured away from the faith.

IN THE SHALLOW WATERS OF DE-CHRISTIANIZATION

You can only swim against the current if you have enough water beneath you. The water level of religious education needs to be raised. There are few countries and cultures in which priests are borne along by an environment that is deeply rooted in a Church to which most of the population belongs. When people receive recognition for striving honestly to fulfill their tasks in the family, at work, and in their involvement in culture and politics to the best of their ability, this private and public respect becomes an incentive to redouble their efforts. People are prepared to make enormous efforts, even as far as giving their lives, if their love meets with a response and understanding. There is no greater frustration than experiencing mockery, indifference, and hatred in response to selfless love. This is Jesus' promise to his messengers, who will be sent like defenseless sheep in the midst of ravening wolves: "Beware of them, [. . .] you will be dragged before governors and kings because of me, as a testimony to them and the Gentiles. [. . .] what you are to say will be given to you at that time; for it is not you who speak, but the Spirit of your Father speaking through you" (Mt 10:16–20).

And the Lord says to his people: "Therefore I send you prophets, sages, and scribes, some of whom you will kill and crucify, and some you will flog in your synagogues and pursue from town to town" (Mt 23:34). But suffering with Christ and in witness to him can also be a blessing to us. For: "Blessed are you when people revile you and persecute you and utter all kinds of evil against you falsely on my account. Rejoice and be glad, for your reward is great in heaven, for in the same way they persecuted the prophets who were before you" (Mt 5:11f.).

In most countries with an originally Christian culture, a dominant ideology of a different hue has established itself, one that is often also openly or subtly aggressive, rejecting Christianity in its substance or despising it as a stage of human development that has been outgrown. There are variations in the means employed in the battle for a substantial de-Christianization of society, its ethics, and its concept of man. But there is unity in the goal.

THE TRANSCENDENTAL BROADENING OF HORIZONS IS SALUTARY

The relativism of postmodernity errs when it considers truth to be altogether unknowable, for if cognition exists at all, then the ontological and epistemological criterion of distinguishing true from false knowledge also exists. This also goes for theories about truth. Likewise, the thesis according to which forgoing the cognition of truth makes it possible for human beings to live together tolerantly, each with his or her own truth, runs counter to experience. In fact the vacuum that results from dispensing with the fundamental questions about God, the world, and mankind is filled by worldviews and political ideologies of a totalitarian nature which inevitably eliminate freedom, too, along with the abandoning of truth.

The greater the observer's remove from Christianity, the smaller the differences are perceived to be between the Catholic Church and the other Christian denominations. For an atheist all religions are the same in that they all portray an undeveloped and pre-scientific self-understanding of man. For a religious person who relates to an apersonal sacred mystery beyond the phenomenal world or even beyond the difference between being and nonbeing, all religions are the same which believe in a personal God. Their differences seem to him to be merely about the manner in which the one God is worshipped. A liberal modernist Christian who sees Christianity as a merely cultural phenomenon is bound to dismiss the teachings on controversial theology proposed by the churches and ecclesial communities as being more akin to expressions of a narrow factionalism and an apodictic understanding of truth. For such a Christian the truth is actually not in itself knowable. Just as the transcendental self does not cognize reality, the "thing in itself," but only its appearances, which it constitutes from its forms of intuition and categories, neither does the religious self know God in the word of his revelation but can only cognize human notions of

God, which may be capable of reflecting his mystery in many different ways but cannot express it clearly in creed and dogma.

OUR MIND HAS A CAPACITY FOR TRUTH

But, after a realistic approach to the world and the fundamental existential questions of our existence, man is quite capable of knowing the truth that manifests itself to him in the being of things and which challenges him in the claim of the good. This means that it is possible for a human being to arrive at the certainty of the existence and power of God in his absolute world transcendence (cf. Rom 1:19f.) by means of a rationally replicable process of proof (demonstratively) based on the fact that the world itself exists at all.

Man is therefore also the hearer of a revelation that has in fact been made and in which God reveals himself to humanity in word and Spirit. Thus, mediated through creation and the Incarnation, man enters into a personal, dialogical, and sacramental community of salvation with God. This is recognized by all Christians relating to Jesus Christ, the Son of God, who took on our humanity. Consequently, even though they depend on the all-embracing mysteries of the Trinity, the Incarnation, and the divinization of man, the differences in conceptions of the historical and gracious mediation of truth and life are not in fact of secondary importance. This is the subject of ecumenical theology. Only in this way can we arrive at an understanding of the sacramental and hierarchical constitution of the Church, her efficacious salvific signs, the apostolic tradition, and her infallible magisterium. Hence the sacramental ordo, too, is not just one ecumenical topic among others. It is crucial for the understanding of the Church as "the universal sacrament of salvation" (*LG* 48; *GS* 45; cf. *LG* 1) in Christ.

And in view of how difficult it is to bring these people back to the faith from which they imagined they had to emancipate themselves, one almost feels like giving up with a sigh of resignation from scripture: "For it is impossible to restore again to repentance those who have once been enlightened, and have tasted the heavenly gift, and have shared in the Holy Spirit, and have tasted the goodness of the word of God and the powers of the age to come, and then have fallen away" (Heb 6:4-6).

And St. Paul's outrage at the speed with which the newly converted abandoned Christ springs even more to mind: "You foolish Galatians! Who has bewitched you? It was before your eyes that Jesus Christ was publicly exhibited as crucified! [. . .] Are you so foolish? Having started with the Spirit, are you now ending with the flesh?" (Gal 3:1–3). But abandoning Christ is not just the result of whatever times and ideologies happen to be contemporary. For the Church of Christ has in principle always had to take into account the warning: "For the time is coming when people will not put up with sound doctrine, but having itching ears, they will accumulate for themselves teachers to suit their own desires, and will turn away from listening to the truth and wander away to myths" (2 Tim 4:3f.).

Even convinced Christians can one day weary of the constant challenge of confessing their faith in Christ. They are tempted to give in to the pressure to conform. Is what lies behind the call for "reform" a readiness for renewal in Christ and the courage to suffer and fight for the truth, or is it just weary resignation before the spirit of the times and the temptation of an easy life?

Jesus' commission to Peter always applies: "Put out into the deep water and let down your nets for a catch" (Lk 5:4)—and that was after they had worked all night long but caught nothing. And in response to Jesus' words we, too, will be prepared to cast out our nets again. And like the apostles we shall catch so many fish that our nets will be beginning to break (cf. Lk 5:6; cf. Jn 21:11).

There are situations of temptation and inner doubt that can bring down even the servants of Jesus Christ. But Christ, too, the high priest of the new and eternal covenant, in whose service we priests stand, can empathize with our weakness, for he, too, was led into temptation. Even the Son of God was not spared the drama of the Mount of Olives. "Let us therefore approach the throne of grace with boldness, so that we may receive mercy and find grace to help in time of need" (Heb 4:16).

If human beings were not capable of being "Hearers of the Word," as runs the title of an important work by Karl Rahner, then there would be no knowledge of God, neither in his revelation in creation nor in the history of salvation. The profession of faith and the symbols of worship would be no more than an encoding of human self-experience, and in their objectivization would be a projection onto an empty transcendence.

Metaphysical skepticism, however, and relativism's—paradoxical—claim to absoluteness admit of God's truth in Christian revelation at most as a partially valid system of religious symbols and functions for coping with contingency. In the end, everyone only has his or her own truth, which in the universal system of mutual tolerance submerges itself in the depths of indifference. The capitalist and socialist political systems never tire of promising us an earthly paradise of material wealth and freedom from spiritual suffering.

CHRIST IS MODERNITY IN PERSON

Christianity does not have to adapt to modernity and struggle to carve out a niche for its survival in postmodernity. For belief in God in Jesus Christ is the true modernity, the non-circumventable topicality of freedom, life, and love. The knowledge of God's universal salvific will in the person and work of Christ cannot be superseded by any progress in empirical-scientific knowledge of the world and in material living conditions; nor can it be undermined by any transcendental reflection on the conditions and limitations of our finite thinking.

Against the Gnostic speculations which wanted to reduce the reality of revelation in the history of salvation to the epistemic status of a reified "fleshly" faith, the inspired Irenaeus of

Lyon stressed the factual nature of Christ's saving work in his anti-Gnostic work (ca. AD 180). Christ came into time, but he brought with him "the fullness of time" (cf. Gal 4:4). The eternal encloses itself in time and embraces it. "For this perishable body must put on imperishability, and this mortal body must put on immortality" (1 Cor 15:53). The eternal that has entered into the world will not be eroded by the ravages of time. And everything positive that now evolves in time becomes a part of the imperishable and in it finds its consummation. God does not negate nature corrupted by sin; instead he heals and perfects it.

"Cognoscite quoniam omnem novitatem attulit semetipsum afferens, qui fuerat annuntiatus. Hoc enim ipsum praedicabatur, quoniam novitas venit innovatura et vivificatura hominem. He brought all novelty, by bringing himself who had been announced. For this very thing was proclaimed beforehand, that a novelty should come to renew and quicken mankind" (*Haer.* 4,34,1).

> Christ the beginning and the end, Alpha and Omega.
> Time and eternity are his.
> *Christus est homo modernissimus.*

The Marxist and liberal critics of religion, as heirs to the rationalist and even more so the empiricist Enlightenment philosophy of the eighteenth century, had wanted to denounce Christianity in the age of totalitarian ideologies as an illusion consoling people with the promise of an imaginary world to come. But in depriving them of this consolation, they have also robbed millions of people of the true consolation that they need.

That is why these social systems, as they exist in reality, arouse an impression of disconsolate hopelessness. In their crude ugliness, the drabness of a socialist *plattenbau* housing estate, the dull unimaginativeness of a Stalinist Palace of Culture, and the cold, soulless ostentatiousness of capitalist temples of mammon all in themselves represent an aesthetic rebuttal of their claim to be able to create the new and happy human being. Paradise is by definition the epitome of a garden of bliss. Up to now, one has sought in vain an earthly paradise in what the political programs of self-redemption have produced in the state and in education. The extermination and labor camps in which millions of people were worked to death were a hell on earth. The hatred of life in Western societies with the killing of the unborn, the old, and the sick is just the outcome of the "death of God" in people's hearts—after which anything goes. Godlessness leads to ugliness. "Fools say in their hearts, 'There is no God.' They are corrupt, they do abominable deeds; there is no one who does good" (Ps 14:1). "[T]hey exchanged the truth about God for a lie and worshipped and served the creature rather than the Creator" (Rom 1:25).

TRUTH IS BEAUTIFUL

Yes, the radiance of truth is beautiful. The truth of the word of God in the faith of the Church shines forth in the Christian worship of God in liturgy and caritas. It is not just in the glorious basilicas of our big cities, but also on the wobbly altar of a hut in the Amazon that the dignity of every single human being and of the community that represents the Body of Christ is recognizable in the liturgy. It is only in relation to God that the balanced relationship between person and community is possible, which without him breaks down into the dialectical contradiction between individualism and collectivism.

When we as Jesus' disciples live in God and God lives in us in the divine virtues of faith, hope, and love, we experience a true fellowship that supports us. "As God's chosen ones, holy and beloved, clothe yourselves with compassion, kindness, humility, meekness, and patience. Bear with one another and, if anyone has a complaint against another, forgive each other; just as the Lord has forgiven you, so you also must forgive. Above all, clothe yourselves with love, which binds everything together in perfect harmony" (Col 3:12–14).

So it is not a question of seeking happiness egomaniacally in oneself, as is the case in Western consumer societies. There are people who are petrified that serving others or even sacrificing their own lives would prevent them from fulfilling themselves and satisfying their "needs." Because Christ was the man for others, everyone can find in this the courage for commitment (cf. Phil 2:1–4). Let us then make the words of the apostle our own: "[I]n humility regard others as better than yourselves. Let each of you look not to your own interests, but to the interests of others" (Phil 2:3f.).

A quite different challenge exists in countries with a totalitarian interpretation of religion in the form of militant Islamism, but also in some sections of Hinduism and Buddhism. If religion essentially means worshipping God, then it is completely incompatible with belief in the One God, the Creator of heaven and earth, to enlist the author of life as the commissioner of its destruction. Religiously justified terrorism is self-contradictory. Either someone is religious, then he is not a terrorist; or if he is a terrorist, then he is not religious.

This is something we as Christians, and especially as pastors of the Church, must keep in mind throughout the world. It is not enough that we can live in relative safety as priests in some countries and are guaranteed religious freedom. We feel ourselves to be in fraternal fellowship with all the millions of Christians who suffer persecution worldwide and pay the price of their faithfulness to Christ with their lives, "those who had been slaughtered for the word of God and for the testimony they had given" (Rev 6:9). Every year many priests, too, give their lives in witness to Christ, in whom alone the universal priesthood of all believers and the priesthood of ordained officeholders are both rooted.

On a worldwide scale, Christianity finds itself caught between fundamentalist "religions" that are prepared to use violence and totalitarian ideologies. Under this enormous pressure, the self-secularization of the Church offers itself as an easy way out. Her own existence is then justified not with her having been established by God but with her usefulness to society. Paul warns the Romans against being conformed to the world and urges them to "be transformed by the renewing of your minds, so that you may discern what is the will of God" (Rom 12:2).

If the Church secularizes herself, it is like the salt that has lost its taste. It will be "trampled underfoot." What good is it now? And what is the point of a lamp under a bushel basket? The Church must be "a city built on a hill [that] cannot be hidden," and the disciples are told: "let your light shine before others, so that they may see your good works and give glory to your Father in heaven" (cf. Mt 5:13–16).

The Church is neither one with the world nor the counterplan to it. But she was founded by Christ as a sign and tool of his salvific will in order to free the world from suffering and violence and mankind from degradation and exploitation, and to redeem humanity from sin, death, and the devil.

The Church has always adapted to various languages, mentalities, and cultures. She owes that to her birth at Pentecost. But that is the precise reason why she is in all nations the one People of God on its way to the common goal of all humanity. She proclaims: "Jesus Christ is the same yesterday and today and for ever" (Heb 13:8). And thus she unites people in the one faith in Jesus the Son of God, "for there is no other name under heaven given among mortals by which we must be saved" (Acts 4:12).

4.

THE MEANING AND AIM OF PRIESTLY MINISTRY

Dear Confreres and Fellow Christians,

In this great existential tribulation, I don't want to fob you off by just referring you to the chapter on the Sacrament of Holy Orders in my handbook *Katholische Dogmatik. Für Studium und Praxis der Theologie*[4] or to the wealth of other publications on the subject.[5] You're sure to find all the biblical and magisterial data you need to know collected there.

But the Spirit of Christ forbids us to call out to a confrere in his plight, as Archimedes once did to the centurion who slayed him: "*Noli turbare circulos meos*—Do not disturb my circles!" As is well known, since Scholasticism the handbooks have treated the following topics from the aspects of scripture, history, and the magisterium: the sacramentality of Holy Orders; the matter and form of its sacramental signs, namely the imposition of hands and the consecratory prayer; the inner graces and apostolic powers conferred; the three degrees of the sacrament, namely episcopate, presbyterate, diaconate; the administers and recipients of the Sacrament of Orders.

But it is not just a matter of informing the intellect; rather it is about understanding with the heart, where all our knowledge is transformed into love. Jesus combined the conferring of the office of universal pastor on Peter with the question about greater love. And as Peter professed the faith of the whole Church in his "You are the Messiah, the Son of the living God" (Mt

16:16), he also speaks from the heart of all of her pastors when he says: "Lord, you know everything; you know that I love you" (Jn 21:17).

IT IS REASONABLE TO BELIEVE

Theology does not amount to nothing more than just an exchange of fixed formulas and dogmas. It is not some kind of higher mathematics for a few specialists. It serves the Church and the faith. It always requires *reductio in mysterium*. There is no such thing as a formula for the world, let alone one for God. Theology is always seeking deeper knowledge, and is fully aware that this journey will go on until the Last Judgment. "For now we see in a mirror, dimly, but then we will see face to face. Now I know only in part; then I will know fully, even as I have been fully known. And now faith, hope, and love abide, these three; and the greatest of these is love" (1 Cor 13:12f.). But it is no mean feat to engage in theology with faith, hope, and love.

Hence, even at the highest level, the magisterium never claims to express once and for all every aspect of the totality of the revealed mystery of the faith. For it is from listening to the word of God that the Church absorbs the fullness of revelation into her overall faith awareness. But neither the individual Christian nor the totality of all the faithful throughout the ages is capable of completely and exhaustively penetrating revelation and thus "reducing it to a concept."

The mystery is greater than human understanding (*analogia fidei*), but not than the divine ideas that determine the cognizability of created things. "*Actus credentis non terminatur ad enuntiabile, sed ad rem*—The act of the believer does not terminate in a proposition, but in a thing. For as in science we do not form propositions, except in order to have knowledge about things through their means, so is it in faith" (Thomas Aquinas, *S.th.* II-II q.1 ad 2). Faith is not just trusting in a feeling, but also a cognizing with reason. By virtue of the natural analogy of being, the light of faith also makes possible an *analogia fidei* (Rom 12:6), which brings out more clearly the inner connectedness of all the mysteries of the faith (*nexus mysteriorum*).

No created intellect can ever adequately comprehend the essence of God, neither in the pilgrim state nor in eternal life (Thomas Aquinas, *S.th.* I-II, q.5 a.4). Nevertheless, through the light of the self-communicating word of God and the gift of the Holy Spirit (Rom 5:5) it is possible to participate in the knowing and loving that subsist in God in the person of the Son and the person of the Holy Spirit. In virtue of being a son or daughter and friend of God, a person who is justified and blessed can in truth arrive at the real beginnings of a knowledge and love of God that will be perfected on seeing God face to face. Nor is this in contradiction to man's nature, wounded as it is by sin, but signifies instead its healing and perfection (Thomas Aquinas, *S.th.* I, q.12 a.2). Neither rationalism nor fideism can do justice to the Catholic understanding of faith. This is why there is in the Catholic Church, also with respect to the Sacrament of Orders, an ongoing process of cognizing its essential requirements and constitutive elements as well as the act of receiving these in a binding fashion in the Church's faith awareness by means of dogmatic definitions. But this assumes it to be a fact that Christ himself instituted the ordination of bishops, priests, and deacons as sacramental "partakers of his consecration and his mission" (*LG* 28).

THE NATURE OF
THE SACRAMENT OF ORDERS

The essence or "real idea" (John Henry Newman) of the Sacrament of Orders is expressed in the words of the risen Lord to his eleven disciples, the apostles:

> "Peace be with you. As the Father has sent me, so I send you." When he had said this, he breathed on them and said to them, "Receive the Holy Spirit. If

you forgive the sins of any, they are forgiven them; if
you retain the sins of any, they are retained."
                                                    —John 20:21–23

In the room of the Last Supper, after washing the disciples' feet,
Jesus had already told them, with Peter at their head, "Very
truly, I tell you, whoever receives one whom I send receives me;
and whoever receives me receives him who sent me" (Jn 13:20).

In different words but with the same meaning of the sacramental priesthood representing Jesus Christ, Jesus says to the
seventy-two who are linked to the circle of the Twelve in participating in his messianic consecration and mission: "Whoever
listens to you listens to me, and whoever rejects you rejects me,
and whoever rejects me rejects the one who sent me" (Lk 10:16).

In the historical development of the Church's faith awareness there is no increase in number of the articles of faith over
time but rather a deeper understanding of their meaning (*analogia fidei*)—which always remains organically connected (*nexus
mysteriorum*) to the totality of the revelation of the one and triune
God (Thomas Aquinas, *S.th.* II-II q.1 a.7).

Vatican II summarizes this:

> Christ, whom the Father has sanctified and sent into
> the world (Jn 10:36), has, through his apostles, made
> their successors, the bishops, partakers of his conse-
> cration and his mission. [. . .] Priests, although they
> do not possess the highest degree of the priesthood,
> and although they are dependent on the bishops in
> the exercise of their power, nevertheless they are
> united with the bishops in sacerdotal dignity. By the
> power of the Sacrament of Orders, in the image of
> Christ the eternal high priest (cf. Heb 5:1–10; 7:24;
> 9:11–28), they are consecrated to preach the gospel
> and shepherd the faithful and to celebrate divine
> worship, so that they are true priests of the New
> Testament. (*LG* 28)

Thanks to the Incarnation and the eschatological sending of the Holy Spirit, the Church of the triune God is the universal sacrament of the world's salvation; this alone makes it possible to comprehend the Christological origin, apostolic descent, and profound spiritual efficacy of the ministry of priests as teachers, pastors, and officiants. If "heaven remains closed" in a transcendental view of the world and mankind, without hope of eternal life, then the ministry of the priest as a servant of the word (Lk 1:2) and witness to the incarnate Logos becomes illogical, indeed downright nonsensical. "If the dead are not raised, 'Let us eat and drink, for tomorrow we die'" (1 Cor 15:32; cf. Is 22:13).

But it is only if a person goes beyond the economic logic that appraises everything according to its price and value and allows himself to be liberated from the straitjacket of immanentism that his inalienable dignity becomes clear to him. Man is worth more than the wages he earns for his work or the price he fetches—in both the real and the figurative sense—at the slave markets of this world. Against the horizon of the transcendence of his intellect and will towards an absolute that is not of this world, he begins to understand that he is "summoned to a higher life" (*GS* 10).

The Church is the witness and prophet of this higher life. A priest is the most adamant champion of human dignity and human rights. No one who believes in God will arrogate to himself the right to judge other people according to their economic worth and thus justify showing contempt for children of the same Heavenly Father, exploiting them, depriving them of their liberty, maiming or even murdering them.

The Church was not founded by Christ in order to pursue her own worldly interests but rather for the sake of the unique interest that God has in each one of his creatures. For we profess of the eternal Son of the Father: *propter nos homines et propter nostram salutem descendit de cælis et incarnatus est.*

"For God so loved the world that he gave his only Son, so that everyone who believes in him may not perish but may have eternal life" (Jn 3:16). The Catholic priest is "one approved by him [God], a worker who has no need to be ashamed, rightly explaining the word of truth" (2 Tim 2:15; cf. 1 Tim 6:11).

What then is "the word of truth" or "sound teaching" that he is to proclaim as "a herald and an apostle and a teacher" (2 Tim 1:11ff.) without being ashamed or fearing the world?

It is the gospel of Jesus Christ, the Son of God (Mk 1:1). The gospel is the message of the event that brought for us the final turn for the better, the message of "God, who saved us and called us with a holy calling, not according to our works but according to his own purpose and grace. This grace was given to us in Christ Jesus before the ages began, but it has now been revealed through the appearing of our Saviour Christ Jesus, who abolished death and brought life and immortality to light through the gospel" (2 Tim 1:8–10). And this word of truth is to be found in "the church of the living God, the pillar and bulwark of the truth" (1 Tim 3:15). Paul writes to the Romans: "For I am not ashamed of the gospel; it is the power of God for salvation to everyone who has faith, to the Jew first and also to the Greek. For in it the righteousness of God is revealed through faith for faith; as it is written, 'The one who is righteous will live by faith'" (Rom 1:16f.).

The bishops and presbyters are servants of Jesus Christ and must take care of the Church as a devoted father takes care of his household (cf. 1 Tim 3:5–7).

Just as Paul was appointed as a witness to Christ, "a herald and an apostle [. . .], a teacher of the Gentiles in faith and truth" (1 Tim 2:7), so, too, his pupils and collaborators in apostolic ministry and then also, as they continue the apostles' mission and authority, the bishops and presbyters should profess that "there is one God; there is also one mediator between God and humankind, Christ Jesus, himself human, who gave himself a ransom for all—this was attested at the right time" (1 Tim 2:5f.).

Is this not the "excellence" of the Catholic priesthood that is repeatedly emphasized by the Second Vatican Council (cf. *PO* 1)?

SERVANTS OF THE NEW COVENANT IN THE HOLY SPIRIT

The apostle boasts that God has made him and his coworkers competent to be "ministers of a new covenant" (2 Cor 3:6). He exercises the "ministry of the Spirit," which leads to life, not the ministry of the letter, which kills. How "much more does the ministry of justification abound in glory" than the "ministry of condemnation" in the Old Covenant (2 Cor 3:9)?

So priests should become aware of the glory of their ministry so that they can cope with the sufferings, insults, and privations that they will inevitably encounter in their sacred vocation. The apostles and their successors are empowered in the Holy Spirit to be "ministers of a new covenant" (2 Cor 3:6) because "the message of reconciliation" (2 Cor 5:19) has been entrusted to them to proclaim. It belongs to the new covenant to make present Jesus' sacrificial self-giving "with his own blood, thus obtaining eternal redemption" (Heb 9:12). Precisely in the ministry of those called to be apostles it must become clear that they are disciples of the betrayed, condemned, and crucified Lord. This distinguishes the office of priest from secular positions of power with their high social prestige in the eyes of man. But from their religious superiors, their bishops, and from the pope as pastor of the universal Church, priests need spiritual strengthening in their faith (cf. Lk 22:32).

Priests—who frequently meet with hostility, come up against a wall of silence, and find themselves derided as being out of touch with the world—are in need of comfort, not paternalism and public reprimand. The bishops in particular, on whom "the fullness of the sacrament of Orders [plenitudo sacramenti ordinis] is conferred" (LG 21), should be an example and pattern to the priests for their spiritual and moral life. Part of this is to offer them reassurance concerning the dogmatic foundations. For if it were not true that the Catholic priesthood originates from Christ and is passed on through its own special sacrament, then, although it could act in its own name, it would not be able to mediate supernatural life in the power of the Holy Spirit. As successors to the apostles, we bishops, together with the priests and deacons, are appointed by God in the Sacrament of Orders "to equip the saints for the work of ministry, for building up the body of Christ" (Eph 4:12).

Vatican II sums this up concisely: "Wherefore the priesthood [. . .] is conferred by that special sacrament; through it priests, by the anointing of the Holy Spirit, are signed with a special character and are conformed to Christ the Priest in such a way that they can act in the person of Christ the Head" (*PO* 2).

THE ONE SACRAMENT IN ITS THREE DEGREES OF ORDINATION

Priests are, together with their bishop, the head of the presbyterium, in the words of Vatican II, "true priests of the New Testament. Partakers of the function of Christ the sole Mediator (1 Tim 2:5), on their level of ministry, they announce the divine word to all. They exercise their sacred function especially in the eucharistic worship or the celebration of the Mass, by which, acting in the person of Christ and proclaiming his Mystery, they unite the prayers of the faithful with the sacrifice of their head and renew and apply in the sacrifice of the Mass until the coming of the Lord (cf. 1 Cor 11:26) the only sacrifice of the New Testament, namely, that of Christ offering himself once for all a spotless Victim to the Father (cf. Heb 9:11–28). For the sick and the sinners among the faithful, they exercise the ministry of alleviation and reconciliation, and they present the needs and the prayers of the faithful to God the Father (cf. Heb 5:1–4). Exercising within the limits of their authority the function of Christ as shepherd and head, they gather together God's family as a brotherhood all of one mind and lead them in the Spirit, through Christ, to God the Father. In the midst of the flock they adore him in spirit and in truth (cf. Jn 4:24). Finally, they labor in word and doctrine (cf. 1 Tim 5:17), believing what they have read and meditated upon in the law of God, teaching what they have believed, and putting in practice in their own lives what they have taught" (*LG* 28).

We can see clearly how by the second half of the first century, the apostolic functions of teaching, governing, and sanctifying had already been transferred to the leaders of the communities, the *episkopoi, presbyteroi,* and *diakonoi.* The official title "presbyter" at first denotes more the rank of leaders whereas *episkopos* is used more for the task of the person in charge of welfare. In the biblical context, the latter becomes a synonym for a shepherd/ pastor. But the term "apostle," too, displays a connection with the names for officeholder of the post-apostolic period. The "episcopacy" taken away from Judas Iscariot is transferred to the subsequently chosen apostle Matthias (Acts 1:20–26). And the apostle Peter, to whom the Lord entrusted the universal care of his lambs and sheep (cf. Jn 21:15–19), addresses himself as a fellow presbyter (1 Pt 5:1) to the shepherds of God's flock, which was entrusted to them, too, by Christ. The faithful are called upon to consider "Jesus, the apostle and high priest of our confession" (Heb 3:1), "the great shepherd of the sheep" (Heb 13:20).

There is a recognizable Christological, apostolic, and ecclesial connection underlying the development of the technical terms to denote the office and determining the direction this takes. It is both senseless and confusing to translate "presbyter" with "elder" because it is not a question of the advantage of age but rather one of the precedence of the responsibility accorded to the office. Presbyters can quite easily be younger than their parishioners.

The college of presbyters has a head, who in the course of linguistic developments in the second century came to be referred to almost exclusively as a bishop, as compared to the presbyters, who now belonged to the second degree. The bishop ranks above the others, not on account of holding a position of greater power in the political sense or as within the organization of a club, but because within the apostolic succession, in which all officeholders participate, he represents the principle of its Christological-vertical and apostolic-horizontal origins. So all presbyters are pastors, but their bishop is the chief pastor. "Thus the divinely established ecclesiastical ministry is exercised on different levels" (*LG* 28). The emerging terminology is more akin to canon law inasmuch as the one apostolic office is exercised "by those who from antiquity have been called bishops, priests [presbyters] and deacons" (*LG* 28). It must be added that bishop and presbyter are combined in the term "priest-*sacerdos*" on account of their inner closeness to Christ, the head of the Church, whom they represent when presiding at the Eucharist.

Even after the emergence of the threefold office of bishop, presbyter, and deacon and despite the different degrees of ordination and powers, what remains crucial is the direct personal relationship of every single officeholder to Christ. The bishop is not the pope's delegate. The priest preaches, governs, and sanctifies his parish in the authority and power of Christ, the true head of the Church, while at the same time recognizing the visible head of the Church in the bishop, too. The "fullness of the sacrament of Orders" (*LG* 21) is conferred on the bishops, so that they sanctify and govern the faithful in the person of the head of the Church. But on their own level the presbyters also participate in the office of mediator and priest of Christ, which they exercise most supremely in the celebration of the eucharistic sacrifice. So in spite of their hierarchical dependence on the bishop they are along with him "(true) priests of the New Testament" (*LG* 28, *PO* 3), who teach, govern, and sanctify in the person of Christ, the head of the Church.

The distinguishing of the degrees of orders in passing on apostolic authority arose from the need for the various ministries in the Church. This has resulted in a system of the many coworkers, who are joined together in the bishop as the principle of the unity of the servants of the Church and the multiplicity of God's coworkers, forming a *communio* of the presbytery and clergy of a diocese. This is why it is the bishop alone who confers orders through prayer and imposition of hands (Thomas

Aquinas, *S.th.* Suppl. q.37 a.5). The bishop possesses the *completio potestatis* over the Church, the Mystical Body of Christ (*S.th.* Suppl. q.38 a.1). In the unity of its origins in the apostolate, the Sacrament of Orders is not, despite the multiple degrees of ordination, something pieced together like parts of a whole. There is only one Sacrament of Orders that is participated in, albeit with graduated degrees of powers imparted. It is a *distinctio totius potestativi* in such a way that the fullness of power is given in one person, namely the bishop, who passes it on to different degrees in the ordination of priests and deacons and in the minor orders.

The fullness of the Sacrament of Orders is realized in the priesthood (according to the orders of bishops and priests), and in the other degrees of ordination within the limits of the powers conferred. Hence, there is only one single Sacrament of Orders but a multiplicity of bearers of it in the different degrees of ordination (Thomas Aquinas, *S.th.* Suppl. q.37 a.1 ad 2). The question of the dogmatic difference between bishop and presbyter and consequently of the sacramentality of episcopal consecration—which remains unclarified in most scholastic authors—is not going to be dealt with here. An answer is in any case only possible by examining more closely how their authority is directed towards the sacramental Body of Christ and the ecclesial Body of Christ. Vatican II decided the question dogmatically by stating that the fullness of the Sacrament of Orders is transmitted "of its very nature" through episcopal consecration (*LG* 21). The bishop's power to ordain and the chief pastor's power of jurisdiction must not be torn apart. In episcopal ordination Christ bestows the authority to preach, to sanctify, and to govern. This is not contradicted by the fact that bishops only exercise their offices of sanctifying, teaching, and governing with the consent of the Roman pontiff (*LG* 22; *Nota praevia explicativa* 2). But the relationship of the pope to the bishops is not like that, for instance, of the Superior General of the Society of Jesus to his provincial superiors or of the Holy See as a subject of international law to the apostolic nuncios. That is why the pope can only appoint bishops or remove them from office as a punishment according to a regulated procedure. Their equality in episcopal orders precludes all arbitrariness, the latter being nothing but harmful to the Church. For the pope is not the lord of the Church and the boss of the bishops, but rather "a permanent and visible source and foundation" of the unity of the universal Church and the whole episcopate in order to serve the truth of the gospel and the Church's teaching (*LG* 18).

THE UNITY OF THE COMMON PRIESTHOOD AND THE SACRAMENTAL PRIESTHOOD IN CHRIST

The relationship between clergy and laity is also not determined by the principle of one ruling over the other, but rather by their unity in the service of the Church for the salvation of the world. Their shared mission is rooted in Baptism, through which we become members of the one Body of Christ, the Church. This shared but also different participation in the priesthood of Christ is where the communion and mission of the Church are carried out: in the priesthood of all the baptized and in that of those ordained in the Sacrament of Orders as pastors of the People of God, that is, the bishops, priests, and deacons.

It was the secret of the success of Reformation preaching that through the "rediscovery" of the universal priesthood the laity felt liberated from religious spoon-feeding by the "hierarchy" of pope and bishops and from having to make financial contributions towards the sacrifice of the Mass, in which the priest alone—for money—appeared to be able to procure the forgiveness of sins for the living and the dead. Now they no longer had to rely on the sacraments and the good will of their ministers. People felt they had personal and direct access to God in faith alone. By flattering the self-esteem and the urge for independence of the "laity," that is, the powerful princes and the burghers in the towns, by telling them that by virtue of the universal priesthood they had direct access to God and no longer required priests as their teachers and shepherds, the Reformers created an anti-hierarchical fervor and fostered alienation from sacramental thinking. This resulted in people wanting to set jealous boundaries between the baptized laity and the priests who allegedly threatened their maturity and freedom of conscience.

The whole pathos of freedom from authority and emancipation from every kind of immaturity that was propagated by Enlightenment philosophy combines with the Reformation's "discovery" of the universal priesthood into a "paradigm shift" and becomes the principle of God's revelation in the passing of history. "World history is the progress of the consciousness of freedom—a progress whose necessity we have to investigate."[6] The Catholic Church, which Hegel identified with medieval feudal society, is Christianity at the stage of exteriority in the necessary progression of the dialectical unfolding of its idea as spirit and freedom. The priest, the saints, the visible rites and ceremonies in Catholicism are—in Hegel's opinion—the expression of the exteriorization of religion and of a mindless performance of cult that binds the spirit to sensual things and subjugates its freedom. "The element of mediation between God and man was thus apprehended and held as something external. Thus through the perversion of the principle of Freedom, absolute Slavery became the established law."[7]

Irrespective of such idealistically extravagant speculations about the self-realization of the absolute spirit as it passes through world history, which renders any search for the unity of all Christians in the one Church redundant, a realistic view from the perspective of salvation history must open up a new appreciation of the sacramentality of the Church, her priesthood, and her liturgy.

The important thing is for the Church, as the "same, identical historical subject" of belief in revelation, to mediate salvation in signs that are perceptible to the senses. Added to this are human beings as ministers and recipients of sacramental grace. All this results from man's nature as body and soul and as a social being, but above all from the Incarnation, which gives invisible grace the visible form of its presence. It follows from God's Incarnation that his humanity is the instrument for the mediation of divine salvation, and that this is done through human beings and in a human manner. "Rightly, then, the liturgy is considered as an exercise of the priestly office of Jesus Christ. In the liturgy the sanctification of the man is signified by signs perceptible to the senses, and is effected in a way which corresponds with each of these signs; in the liturgy the whole public worship is performed by the Mystical Body of Jesus Christ, that is, by the Head and his members" (*SC* 7).

In the Catholic Church, priests and laity are not opposites in closed groups as in an estates-based society. Notwithstanding sociological alienations of the Church's constitution over the course of history, the ecclesiologically correct formulation must run: "In the Church there is a diversity of ministry but a oneness of mission. Christ conferred on the apostles and their successors the duty of teaching, sanctifying, and ruling in his name and power. But the laity likewise share in the priestly, prophetic, and royal office of Christ and therefore have their own share in the mission of the whole people of God in the Church and in the world" (*AA* 2).

Although these ideas of the laity's being dependent on the arbitrary behavior of the priests were in circulation in the fifteenth century, they were in fact the result of both a lack of knowledge of the faith on the part of the laity and negligent or incompetent teachers. The fact that the whole of the missionary People of God have been endowed with a priestly dignity and mission (1 Pt 2:5, 9) is not inconsistent with the ministry of the presbyters together with the apostles as shepherds of the faithful in the name of Christ, "the chief shepherd" (1 Pt 5:4) and "the shepherd and guardian of your souls" (1 Pt 2:25). The ministry of the presbyters as shepherds is clearly derived from Christ, who governs, teaches, and sanctifies his Church through them. Incidentally, there is no talk here of a "common" or "universal" priesthood and certainly not of a contrast between this and a presumptive "special" priesthood. When the Church's holy and royal priesthood is spoken of, this refers to a characteristic of the holiness of God's people (cf. Ex 19:6) as a temple of God "to offer spiritual sacrifices acceptable to God through Jesus Christ" (1 Pt 2:5; cf. Rev 1:6; 20:6) and is a statement of the Church's priestly mission to "proclaim the mighty acts" of God (1 Pt 2:9) to the people.

PRIESTS AND LAITY UNITED IN THE SACRIFICE OF CHRIST AND THE CHURCH

"Therefore be imitators of God, as beloved children, and live in love, as Christ loved us and gave himself up for us, a fragrant offering and sacrifice to God" (Eph 5:1f.). This gives us the Christological and Christian definition of sacrifice: the essence of the sacrifice is love as the surrender of one's whole being and life to God, from whom we have received everything (sacrifice of thanksgiving) and from whom we hope everything (sacrifice of supplication). Perfect love of God makes the sacrifice of love of neighbor possible.

God, the Creator of the world, "who has blessed us in Christ with every spiritual blessing" (Eph 1:3), has no need of propitiation with gifts of the world, which is anyway his creation. In the Eucharist the bishop or presbyter, together with all the faithful, offers the sacrifice of thanksgiving in which the reconciliation with God granted us once and for all in Jesus Christ is now made present in the liturgical sign and the surrender of our hearts. This thanksgiving is not a matter of external applause for someone else's successful achievement. Rather, it is an entering into, indeed a uniting with, the thanksgiving that Jesus is in his person for the receipt of his divine nature and the inclusion of all mankind in his human nature through faith and baptism. Thus Christ is one with the Church as her Head and Body. The criticism of cult expressed both in the Old Testament and by Jesus is not incompatible with the sacramental memorial of Jesus' Passion that he commanded the disciples at the Last Supper to perform. "The oblation of the Church, therefore, which the Lord gave instructions to be offered throughout all the world, is accounted with God a pure sacrifice, and is acceptable to Him; not that He stands in need of a sacrifice from us, but that he who offers is himself glorified in what he does offer, if his gift be accepted" (Irenaeus of Lyon, *Haer.* 4,18,1).

Since the bishop as shepherd and teacher, but also when presiding at the liturgy, acts in the person of Christ, the high priest of the new covenant, he is also referred to as a high priest: "For if Jesus Christ, our Lord and God, is Himself the chief priest of God the Father, and has first offered Himself a sacrifice to the Father, and has commanded this to be done in commemoration of Himself, certainly that priest truly discharges the office of Christ, who imitates that which Christ did; and he then offers a true and full sacrifice in the Church to God the Father, when he proceeds to offer it according to what he sees Christ Himself to have offered" (Cyprian of Carthage, *Epistle* 62, 14). In the oldest extant complete ordination ritual, which has been handed down to us by Hippolytus (ca. 200), the bishop is called a high priest because he offers the gifts of the Church as thanksgiving to the Father through Christ in the Holy Spirit (*TA* 3): this term *hiereus/sacerdos* later comes to comprise both degrees of ordination, both the episcopate and the presbyterate, and links them closely together. The fact that all the faithful are called "priests of God and of Christ" (Rev 20:6) in no way passes into oblivion.

In his *City of God* Augustine, too, describes the subject universally familiar to subsequent ecclesial and theological tradition in order to justify the common priesthood of all the faithful and the ministerial priesthood of bishops and presbyters: "and this [being priests of God] refers not to the bishops alone, and presbyters, who are now specially called priests in the Church (*qui proprie iam vocantur in ecclesia sacerdos*); but as we call all believers Christians on account of the mystical chrism, so we call all priests because they are members of the one Priest (*sic omnes sacerdotes, quoniam membra sunt unius sacerdotis*). Of them the Apostle Peter says, 'A holy people, a royal priesthood'" (*Civ.* 10,10).

This inner connection established by Augustine between the priesthood of all believers and the priestly-sanctifying ministry of bishops and priests by virtue of their sharing in the one priesthood of Christ is again taken up by Vatican II in *Lumen Gentium* 10:

> Though they differ from one another in essence and not only in degree, the common priesthood of the faithful and the ministerial or hierarchical priesthood are nonetheless interrelated: each of them in its own special way is a participation in the one priesthood of Christ. The ministerial priest, by the sacred power he enjoys, teaches and rules the priestly people; acting in the person of Christ, he makes present the eucharistic sacrifice, and offers it to God in the name of all the people. But the faithful, in virtue of their royal priesthood, join in the offering of the Eucharist. They likewise exercise that priesthood in receiving the sacraments, in prayer and thanksgiving, in the witness of a holy life, and by self-denial and active charity.

As Thomas Aquinas, one of the most reliable witnesses to Catholic tradition, says: "As to the priests of the New Law, they may be called mediators of God and men, inasmuch as they are the ministers of the true Mediator by administering, in His stead, the saving sacraments to men" (*S.th.* III q.26 a.1 ad 1). "Moreover, they fulfill the office of mediator, *non quidem principaliter et perfective, sed ministerialiter et dispositive*" (Thomas Aquinas, *S.th.* III q.26 a.2). This also holds true when speaking of Christ as the sole head of the Church and the bishops as head of their local churches and the pope as visible head of the whole Church. "Now the interior influx of grace is from no one save Christ, Whose manhood, through its union with the Godhead, has the power of justifying; but the influence over the members of the

Church, as regards their exterior guidance, can belong to others. [. . .] First, inasmuch as Christ is the Head of all who pertain to the Church in every place and time and state; but all other men are called heads with reference to certain special places, as bishops of their Churches. Or with reference to a determined time as the Pope is the head of the whole Church, viz. during the time of his Pontificate" (*S.th.* III q.8 a.6). The bishops are pastors because they visibly exercise the pastoral office of Christ whereas only Christ calls himself the door, for it is only through him that we can really enter the house of God (cf. Augustine, *Tr. in Io.* 46). Certain titles and verbal images for Christ can also be applied analogously to his servants (shepherd, teacher, priest, mediator); others apply univocally and exclusively to him (Word made flesh, Bread of Life, Light of the World, Redeemer).

5.

THE SACRAMENTAL PRIESTHOOD UNDER THE SCRUTINY OF REFORMATION CRITICISM

Dear Confreres and Fellow Christians,

The great crisis of the Catholic priesthood in the sixteenth century has been frequently talked about.

Ultimately, the "Reformation" that was set in motion by Martin Luther (1483–1546) gave rise to "Protestantism" (in its various forms) as an alternative concept of Christianity as opposed to the Catholic Church. Unlike Protestantism, the Catholic Church does not define herself in contrast to another denomination but rather through her identity with the Church of the apostles. She has no desire to nor can she understand herself as a denomination analogous to Lutheran, Zwinglian, Calvinist, Methodist, or Anglican denominations.

> Christ, the one Mediator, established and continually sustains here on earth his holy Church, the community of faith, hope and charity, as an entity with visible delineation [. . .]. This is the one Church of Christ which in the Creed is professed as one, holy, catholic

and apostolic, which our Saviour, after his Resurrection, commissioned Peter to shepherd (Jn 21:17) and him and the other apostles to extend and direct with authority (cf. Mt 28:18–20) which he erected for all ages as "the pillar and mainstay of the truth" (1 Tim 3:15). This Church constituted and organized in the world as a society, subsists in the Catholic Church, which is governed by the successor of Peter and by the bishops in communion with him, although many elements of sanctification and of truth are found outside of its visible structure. These elements, as gifts belonging to the Church of Christ, are forces impelling toward catholic unity. (*LG* 8)

Quite apart from legitimate variations in forms of piety, the new form of Christianity that came out of the sixteenth-century Reformation differs from the Catholic Church that preceded and followed it not just in individual doctrines and essential elements of its sacramental constitution. This had previously been the case for 1,500 years with many heretical groupings, and likewise with the revocation of communion with the Eastern Churches, as well as the schisms and the development of sects in the High and Late Middle Ages.

A NEW FORM OF CHRISTIANITY?

A new basic understanding came about. It did not concern revelation as such or the mysteries of the Trinity and the Incarnation or salvation as divine grace; rather, it was precisely about the understanding of the ecclesial and sacramental mediation of grace and hence the constitution and mission of the Church. The formal and material principles (*sola scriptura, sola fide, sola gratia*) are in tension with the formulations of Catholic identity of the kind formulated by Irenaeus of Lyon in the second century against Gnosticism. In the mutually referential context of sacred scripture, apostolic tradition, and the apostolic succession of all legitimate bishops and of the Bishop of Rome as the successor to

Peter, the word of God as found in the teachings of the apostles is faithfully interpreted and preserved in its entirety. The *doctrina apostolorum* is identical with how it is passed on in the *depositum fidei* and thus with the binding doctrine of the Catholic Church.

When the teaching authority of the Church is missing from this structure, the dynamic unity of scripture and tradition, in fact even the unity of scripture itself, collapses. Ultimately it becomes impossible to make sense any longer of the unity of Jesus and the Church of the apostles at the level of faith as well. Historical research alone can neither provide a formal guarantee of the Creed nor reconstruct its contents. It has no more to offer than hypotheses.

The synthesis of a historical and a dogmatic approach to divine revelation in Christ is characteristic of the way hermeneutics works in Catholic theology. Augustine already expressed this in his famous formulation against the Manichaeans (397): "*Ego vero Evangelio non crederem, nisi me Catholicae Ecclesiae commoveret auctoritas*" (Contra epistolam quam vocant Fundamenti 5,6). There is no need at all for us to attempt to jump from one side of the "ugly, broad ditch" to the other on account of Gotthold Ephraim Lessing and his "necessary truths of reason" and "accidental truths of history."[8] The barque of St. Peter sails gently along in the middle of the stream towards the harbor.

The fact that the sacramentality of the Church is present in a condensed form in the sacramental priesthood of bishop and presbyter inevitably led to fierce controversy on precisely this issue. The matter has to this day not been satisfactorily resolved and separates the Catholic and Orthodox Churches on the one hand and the ecclesial communities belonging to the Reformed tradition on the other. At issue is the dogmatic question of the nature of the sacramental priesthood.

A DOGMATIC DIFFERENCE

The dogmatic content of the priesthood must be clearly differentiated from time-conditioned structures and especially from the moral impropriety of individual persons and their lack of pastoral zeal. The controversy between Catholics and Protestants over ministry is, after all, of a dogmatic nature.

After 500 years, we now have to clear away the debris that has piled up in the meantime as a result of polemics and the malicious distortion of other positions in order to clarify our differences in an ecumenical spirit and, if possible, to overcome them or at least get back to what really lies at the heart of them.

In his 1520 treatise *On the Babylonian Captivity of the Church*, Luther completely denied the existence of the Sacrament of Holy Orders. He declared it to be an invention of the Church and the pope, who is in his opinion the Antichrist (*WA* 6,560). He argued that it was not instituted by Christ and therefore did not promise the grace of forgiveness of sins and that it was not constitutive for the justification of the sinner. Luther contends that maintaining the indelible character of priesthood has established two estates of Christians, which goes both against the universal priesthood of all Christians that results from Baptism and, consequently, against direct access to God for all who are justified in faith and in conscience. "For whatever issues from baptism may boast that it has been consecrated priest, bishop and pope"—so runs Luther's famous formulation in his address *To the Christian Nobility of the German Nation* (*WA* 6,408).

The argument goes that, through the fiction of a sacrament of ordination, the ministry of the word has turned into an exploitative rule of priests over the laity, which contradicts true Christian brotherhood. Luther traces ordination back to the rite of choosing a member of the community to be a preacher and custodian of the sacraments; this person would then *publicly* exercise the priesthood of all the baptized in the name of the community. In his view, no essential difference exists between the priest and the members of the community as a result of a *character indelebilis* impressed on the former in ordination. This "indelible seal" means that a person is entrusted permanently with priestly ministry, so that he can act in the person of Christ, as head of his Body, in the name of the Church. Hence it is

Christ himself who leads and sanctifies the community through the ordained priest. For this reason, there is for Luther only one priesthood, namely that conferred in Baptism. Everyone belongs to the religious estate. In his address *To the Christian Nobility of the German Nation* (1520), Luther states that the difference between "priests" and laity is merely functional. Bishops and priests are merely representatives mandated by the community, and where they preach and baptize they do so by virtue of the spiritual powers communicated to everyone in Baptism.

> For whatever issues from baptism may boast that it has been consecrated priest, bishop, and pope, although it does not beseem everyone to exercise these offices. For, since we are all priests alike, no man may put himself forward or take upon himself, without our consent and election, to do that which we have all alike power to do. For, if a thing is common to all, no man may take it to himself without the wish and command of the community. And if it should happen that a man were appointed to one of these offices and deposed for abuses, he would be just what he was before. Therefore a priest should be nothing in Christendom but a functionary; as long as he holds his office, he has precedence over others; if he is deprived of it, he is a peasant and a citizen like the rest. Therefore a priest is verily no longer a priest after deposition. But now they have invented *caracteres indelebiles* and pretend that a priest after deprivation still differs from a simple layman. (*WA* 6,408)

The denial of the Catholic ordained priesthood and the establishment of a new office in line with the Lutheran view of the universal priesthood brought with it a change in terminology, too. Although the German word *"Priester"* (English *priest*; French *prêtre*; Old French *prestre*) is derived from the biblical *presbyteros*, it had, when used in connection with the sacrifice of the Mass, taken on the connotation of a sacerdotal mediator between God and man; this then came to be supplanted more and more by the concept of the Protestant predicant. The predicant is the preacher of the pure gospel and the custodian of the sacraments, which are celebrated in faithful accordance with their institution. In the Lutheran national churches of Scandinavia and also in the Anglican Church, the traditional terms of *bishop*, *priest*, and *deacon* have been retained. Nonetheless the description of their essence is altered. Where the biblical title of "pastor" has been retained, this has to this day maintained a terminological bridge between the denominations. In German, the canonical term *"Pfarrer"* is used by both Catholics and Protestants. In English, the term "pastor" is widely used by Protestants, and in the USA also by Catholics, too, while "parish priest" is used in some non–Roman Catholic denominations as well as by Catholics. In Catholic canon law, the parish priest is an ordained priest who is put in charge of a parish or pastoral unit. In German Protestant usage, *"Pfarrer"* is the official title for an ordained preacher; in English, *pastor, minister, preacher, parson,* and *vicar* are among the terms used for the person in charge of a parish.

Protestant ordination means being appointed to an ecclesial office—quite possibly with spiritual powers and with a blessing through imposition of hands by a higher member of the clergy. Catholic ordination by contrast is understood as a consecratory and sacramental act through which the image of Christ the Priest is imprinted so deeply on the soul of the person ordained that, in the power of the Holy Spirit, he preaches, baptizes, offers the Church's sacrifice, forgives sins, etc., all in the person of Christ.

Despite these great differences, not every analogy between the consecrated Catholic priesthood and the ordained Protestant preaching office is lost. In fact, a relatively broad correspondence still exists at least as far as the tasks of preaching, administering the sacraments as means of grace, and leading the parish as its pastor in Christ's name are concerned. That is also the reason why the Catholic Church can in certain circumstances dispense former Protestant pastors from mandatory celibacy and ordain them as priests.

Although it is to be noted that Luther later put the emphasis of ordination more on its role in keeping order in the parish so as to combat the disorderliness of the "enthusiasts," the fundamental difference still lies in the grounds given for the powers it confers. Are they already communicated to every Christian by virtue of Baptism even though they cannot be exercised without a mandate from the community, or are they—presupposing "the sacraments of Christian initiation"—"conferred by that special sacrament" (*PO* 2)?

If one wishes to call the rite a sacrament, as Melanchthon was later still to do (*CA* 13), then this, they argue, is merely a matter of the ministers of word and sacrament being properly called, not a matter of a sacrificial priesthood as a continuation of the Levitical priesthood—something no one had anyway ever maintained.

What is happening here is that a conclusion is being drawn about the sacramental priesthood from the understanding of the Mass as the sacramental making present of the sacrifice of the Cross. This then assumes that the sacramental priesthood is about offering God further sacrifices for the sins of the living and the dead in addition to and after Christ's one redemptive sacrifice on the Cross. This is what is imputed to the Catholic faith in the *Confessio Augustana* (1530) and its *Apology* (Art. 24). Catholic doctrine is misinterpreted as meaning that Christ offered the sacrifice on the Cross for original sin and the sins of all who had hitherto lived, meaning that the sacrifice of holy Mass would have to be offered over and over again for the sins of mankind by the priests as new mediators alongside Christ, the one and only priest of the new covenant (*CA* 24). In reality, the liturgical celebration of the Mass makes sacramentally present the all-reconciling sacrifice of the Cross. "This sacrament is called a 'Sacrifice' inasmuch as it re-presents the Passion of Christ—*hoc sacramentum dicitur sacrificium, inquantum repraesentat ipsam passionem Christi*" (Thomas Aquinas, *S.th.* III q.73 a.4 ad 3).

THE SACRIFICE OF THE MASS AND THE PAPACY AS OBJECTS OF LUTHER'S ENMITY

"Priesthood" and the "sacrifice of the Mass" are for Luther the epitome of self-justification or righteousness through works. He sees in this combination the reason for the perversion of the "Popish church." Hence the pope is for him the Antichrist, and the Mass is "the greatest and most horrible abomination" and "above and before all other popish idolatries" (*Smalcald Articles* II, 2). He views the Catholic priesthood as regression to the Old Testament priesthood, or even as an apostasy into a pagan sacrificial priesthood. As he says in the *Smalcald Articles* (1537) against the planned Council of Mantua, this "directly conflicts with the chief article," namely that the minister is justified through grace by faith alone. Instead of receiving grace in faith as a gift (*donum*), the Mass has in Luther's eyes been turned into a work of men and their sacrifice (*sacrificium*) for God. From this he deduces that the Mass as a sacrifice is the epitome of turning the order of salvation into its opposite. For it is not the priest as "a wicked or a godly hireling of the Mass with his own work, but the Lamb of God and the Son of God that takes away our sins" (*Smalcald Articles* II, 2). And his conclusion is:

> This article concerning the Mass will be the whole business of the Council. For if it were possible for them to concede to us all the other articles, yet they could not concede this one. [. . .] They feel well enough that when the Mass falls, the Papacy lies in ruins. (*Smalcald Articles* II, 2)

These statements constitute the correct conclusion drawn from a premise that we Catholics regard as false. As a result of his idea of *natura totaliter corrupta*, Luther sees divine and human action to be totally opposed. Man can only receive grace but cannot himself, by virtue of being commissioned by Christ and empowered by the Holy Spirit, become a living instrument for the passing on of the grace of redemption. However, from a Catholic point of view, original sin does not mean that man's substance has been transformed into the substance of sin. Man's striving nature is identical with his creatureliness. It follows then that even when governed by sin, by no means all the virtues of pagans are vices and all their philosophical-anthropological knowledge errors or lies. That is why we adhere to the continuity of the individual and his or her personal identity in a state of grace, of original sin, and of redemption.

THE PRIOR METHODOLOGICAL DECISION DETERMINED THE INTERPRETATION

It was as a result of the abuses in the Church's salvific ministry, as Luther sees them, or premised on such misunderstandings, as the Catholic side would put it, that the whole biblical witness, too, was read in different ways: either in contrast to patristic and scholastic tradition or in an attempt to display the unity of the two. A hermeneutic of rupture and discontinuity is an obstacle to a hermeneutic of unity and continuity. So it came about that Protestant and Catholic theologians and Church historians, using the same biblical and patristic sources, for 500 years constructed opposite lines of argumentation, all of them intended to put the respective opposite side in the wrong. This does, however, show how an unreflected prior understanding in dogmatics was bound to result in contradictory interpretations of the origins, development, and depiction of the essence of the apostolic office.

Not a single dogmatic document of the Church derives the hierarchical priesthood of bishop and presbyter from the Levitical priesthood of the Old Testament. And in terms of the history of religion it would be completely out of the question for the sacrifices as a propitiation of the gods through human

oblations would be taken into consideration. To be distinguished
from these are the paraenetic admonishments that remind the
bishops and presbyters of the dignity and sacredness of their
ministry (cf. *1 Clem* 42–44) or confront them with prophetic
threats against bad servants of the sanctuary and "you shepherds
of Israel who have been feeding yourselves" (Ezek 34:2). Quite
generally, the stressing of the dignity and glory of the sacrificial
priesthood has, ever since the writings of the Fathers, served not
the priests' sense of superiority but rather their humility. The
superhuman dignity of the priesthood is meant to bring home
to priests the discrepancy between the demands of their office
and the weakness of its human bearers.

John Chrysostom, who wanted to justify his flight from ordination with his treatise *De sacerdotio* (ca. AD 385), makes the comparison of the priest with an angel that had such a long-lasting
influence: "Not an angel but the Paraclete vested in men still
abiding in the flesh this fearful and awful ministry of celebrating
the Eucharistic sacrifice and forgiving sins in his name" (*De sac.*
III, 4). Therefore, similarly: "Great is the Mystery and great
the dignity of priests to whom is given that which has not been
granted the angels" (Thomas à Kempis, *The Imitation of Christ*,
V). And the sacrifice of the Mass is not a sacrifice through which
God is propitiated by human beings, but rather the sacrament
in which—according to Christ's words of institution—the reconciliation with him brought about by God "in the Blood of
Christ" is bestowed concretely on those now participating in
the celebration. In the sacraments, the Church accomplishes
through her head the supreme glorification of God and thus
receives his grace. A devotional work that is above all suspicion
and reflects pre-Reformation spirituality says of the ministry that
the priest receives through the imposition of the bishop's hands:
"For priests alone, rightly ordained in the Church (*rite in ecclesia
ordinatus*), have power to celebrate Mass and consecrate the Body
of Christ. The priest, indeed, is the minister of God, using the
word of God according to His command and appointment.
God, moreover, is there—the chief Author and invisible Worker

to whom all is subject as He wills, to whom all are obedient as He commands."[9] Here, then, the priest is God's instrument.

In the *Catechismus Romanus* (1566), which is based on the teachings of the Council of Trent, priests are called mediators in the sense of interpreters and ambassadors (*Dei interpretes et nuntii*) of another (*Cat. Rom.* II, 7,2). The presbyter, who is sometimes also called *sacerdos*, dedicated to the sacred, because he serves the holy sacraments, is therefore not a mediator and intercessor for the secular rank and file to a higher power and deity in a way that would correspond to the pagan concept. Through his preaching of the gospel, he communicates to successive generations the grace of Christ accomplished once and for all in the history of salvation (*Cat. Rom.* II, 7,22).

The Council of Florence (1439), in its Decree for the Armenians, describes the effect of the Sacrament of Holy Orders conferred by the bishop as "an increase of grace so that one might be a suitable minister of Christ" (DH 1326). Vatican II states equally succinctly: "Those of the faithful who are consecrated by Holy Orders are appointed to feed the Church in Christ's name with the word and the grace of God" (*LG* 11).

The Reformers' concern to emphasize the equal dignity of Christians in the whole Church's priestly ministry is to be welcomed. This does not, however, require making a dogmatic contrast between the royal priesthood of all believers and the ordained priesthood. For when all Christians are called priests, this is not intended to be a reference to the priestly ministry of their shepherds. It is not that something specific is being generalized here; it is simply referring to a characteristic of the Church, the royal People of God. The common priesthood of all the faithful is an ecclesiological statement, not one regarding the theology of office. The best explanation of the connection and difference between the common priesthood of the whole Church and the priestly ministry of bishops and presbyters has been given us by St. Augustine: "For you I am a bishop, with you, after all, I am a Christian" (Sermo 340,1, cf. 340,4), and "I do not want to enter heaven without you" (Sermo 17,2).

For it is in relation to Christ, the Head of the Body, that the connection lies between the common priesthood of all believers and their priestly pastors, namely as participating in different ways in Christ's threefold office of Prophet, Priest, and King. The ecclesial distinction between "laity and priests" (cf. already *1 Clem* 40,5) is, then, something totally different from the social stratification into educated and uneducated, rulers and subjects in feudal society and the later *Ständestaat*, the society of estates. And the reason why the priest is a mediator is certainly not that he is an intermediary between an immature and dependent laity and God and that they would remain distant from God without him. The "immediacy" to God the Father through Christ in the Holy Spirit in prayer and conscience does not run counter to the mediation in the sacraments and priestly ministry. Only God himself is immediate to God. We creatures require mediation into immediacy to God through Christ, the God-Man, and in him through his sacraments and the persons he takes into his service.

As servants of Christ and of the Church, the priests naturally have need of the sacraments themselves, too, and of the priests who administer them. In private personal prayer as well as in the sacramental signs and in the sermon that is listened to devoutly, every spiritual activity that people engage in is communicated through the outer and inner senses. In the sacraments, too, the Christian encounters Jesus Christ personally in the sacraments themselves as well as in the person of the ordained priest, who merely visibly represents Christ as the head of the Church. In each of these different ways, it is all about the one unique presence of Christ, the true Mediator of human beings into immediacy to the triune God (cf. *SC* 7).

What for a long time prevented the great Cardinal John Henry Newman (1801–1890) from converting to the Catholic faith was the Reformed, and also Anglican, preconception that the sacraments, the priests, the saints, and Mary intruded themselves as mediators between God and the soul. But then he recognized, as he wrote in his *Apologia pro vita sua*, "that the Catholic

Church allows no image of any sort, material or immaterial, no dogmatic symbol, no rite, no sacrament, no Saint, not even the Blessed Virgin herself, to come between the soul and its Creator. It is face to face, '*solus cum solo*,' in all matters between man and his God. He alone creates; He alone has redeemed; before His awful eyes we go in death; in the vision of Him is our eternal beatitude" (Chap. IV §2).

A HISTORICAL MISUNDERSTANDING ABOUT THE PRIESTHOOD?

This complete distortion of Catholic doctrine was historically the breaking point at which many Catholics separated themselves from the Catholic Church and "Protestants" newly organized themselves as "the true catholic church reformed according to the Gospel." Tragic though this separation was historically, the observation itself is actually positive for ecumenism. At heart, the Western schism is based, as far as dogmatics is concerned, on a huge misunderstanding, something that is easier to overcome than truly contradictory dissent. It does, after all, offer the possibility of a responsibly sought convergence.

What appear to me to present more difficulties are the different understandings of the concept of justifying faith along with the resultant attitude towards the efficacy of the sacraments. The justification of the sinner through grace is beyond all doubt. But grace does not eliminate the need for participation on the part of the creature; rather, it moves the creature to activate his or her God-given capacities. For grace presupposes nature; it heals and raises up the human being, who is wounded by sin and at the mercy of eternal death. Grace, as it were, unlocks the intellectual and moral energies of human nature again and heightens its strength. The all-embracing efficacy of grace does not contradict the need for the will to freely accept it and with its help to become a genuine "collaborator in building up the Kingdom of God." The dynamic connection between grace and human activity cannot be expressed more beautifully than in the words of St. Augustine: "He who created you without you will not justify you without you" (Sermo 169,11.13). In order to safeguard the omni-efficacy of grace there is no need whatsoever to introduce the idea of the total depravity of nature, which denies mankind, under the rule of Adam's sin, any propensity for good. For sin can indeed sever the supernatural relationship with God in grace, but it cannot destroy man's God-created nature and the working of its spirit and freedom. Since God created man for himself, the natural dependency on transcendence endures in the spirit-gifted creature, even in spite of sin, and expresses itself in a veritable crying out for redemption.

If for Luther the act and content of faith are reduced to the assurance of possessing it and thus knowing oneself to be justified, this leaves the sacraments, as it were, hanging in the air. They are just auxiliary spiritual and psychological supports. But they can no longer be understood as efficacious signs of the mediation of grace. Nevertheless Luther did in some way hold on to the concept of the objective efficacy of the sacraments; otherwise he would not have been able to speak of the objective efficacy of infant baptism by virtue of its being performed. There cannot, after all, be any serious question of a child's possessing a comprehensive and reflective faith. It is in the faith of the Church and the parents and godparents that in Baptism the child is freed from original sin and receives the grace of being a child of God. Luther, however, leaves it open how these opposing positions are to be reconciled, and in fact they do not seem to be reconcilable. If justification by faith alone is defined strictly, then the sacraments cannot but appear to be mere auxiliary supports which as such cannot objectively bring about salvation because this would curtail faith as the sole ground for assurance of salvation.

The Catholic understanding of the objective efficacy of the sacraments for salvation is directed against Donatism, which had made the efficacy of the sacraments dependent on the subjective sanctity of the recipient or the human minister of them. What is meant is not the sacramental (verbal and material) sign that effectively grants the individual the salvation brought about once and for all by Christ; rather, it is Christ himself, who nevertheless makes use of the sacraments that he himself instituted as instruments and of the priests to transmit them. Thus the sacraments are instrumentally efficacious and necessary for salvation (*de necessitate medii et praecepti*).

If, on account of the Incarnation, Christ's human nature is the effective medium through which salvation is realized and mediated, then in it the sacraments that depend on Christ's human nature are no more a false prop of salvation in the creaturely than is Christ's humanity itself. The sacraments and holy Mass as the sacrifice of Christ and the Church cannot be accused of being works of piety (*Werkfrömmigkeit*). For Christ's humanity and the human signs in the sacraments are *media salutis* appropriate to man as a being with body and soul and grounded in the human nature of Christ as the organ of his divine salvific will.

For Christ's high priesthood draws its redeeming power from the divinity of the Son of the Father (Heb 1:2), but it is realized in the humanity of Christ. "Since, therefore, the children share flesh and blood, he himself likewise shared the same things [. . .]. Therefore he had to become like his brothers and sisters in every respect, so that he might be a merciful and faithful high priest in the service of God, to make a sacrifice of atonement for the sins of the people. Because he himself was tested by what he suffered, he is able to help those who are being tested" (Heb 2:14–18).

Although the priesthood that serves the new covenant is not in any way (in either form or content) a continuation of the Levitical priesthood but was merely prefigured in it, a similar relationship obtains, *mutatis mutandis*, in the solidarity that bishops and priests as servants of Christ have with the faithful in their situation of temptation and sin: Christ did not choose angels as his priests but human beings who make present in the manner of human beings the salvific work he accomplished as a human being: "Every high priest chosen from among mortals is put in charge of things pertaining to God on their behalf, to offer gifts and sacrifices for sins" (Heb 5:1).

In its Decree on Justification (13.01.1547) the Council of Trent rejected the reduction of faith to an assurance of justification that rests on nothing else but confidence (*fiducia*) that one is justified for Christ's sake (DH 1562–1564). As nature wounded by original sin is healed, the selflessness of love is possible. Wounded nature—and even less so healed nature with its capacity for striving in spirit and will—is far from being capable only of egoistic self-love. Hence not every good work of pagans is a vice, and it is certainly not true that in every good work the just man sins (so Pope Leo X against Luther: DH 1481). Faith therefore does not consist solely in the certain assurance of being justified but rather in the love that is at work in it (cf. Gal 5:6) and which unites us with God.

Justification in Baptism and in the post-baptismal forgiveness of sins in the Sacrament of Reconciliation presupposes faith as a knowledge of Christ and profession of him; but justification is effectively mediated through the sacraments. All seven sacraments are not merely external signs of the justification already received in fiduciary faith; rather, they are efficacious signs which objectively confer what they signify on the individual believer and the Church now assembled (DH 1606).

FLUID TERMINOLOGY INCREASED THE DIFFICULTY OF DEFINING THE ESSENCE OF PRIESTHOOD

The fact that the terminology is still in a state of flux continues to affect the whole topic and threatens to confuse what is in itself a clear situation. It is correct that the Greek term *hiereus*, to which the Latin *sacerdos* corresponds, is not used to refer to either apostles or presbyters. Where these terms are applied to Christ and the totality of the faithful, it is not with the Levitical priesthood in mind. And it is quite out of the question to impute any relationship with the so-called pagan priesthood either here or later when this title is applied to bishops and presbyters on account of the sacrifice of the Eucharist. The worship of God within the biblical context absolutely precludes the cultic worship of a pagan deity. After all, the foreign gods and idols are merely personifications of created forces which can never be worshipped instead of the Creator. Nor can sacrifices be made to them. No formal or contentual connection exists between the sacrifice of the Mass and either the sacrifices as understood in the history of religion or the quite different type of sacrifice offered by the Levitical priesthood in God's people.

A formal relationship does, however, exist anthropologically to the sacrifice that results from man's created nature. This is a sacrifice of thanksgiving to the Creator for life and its preservation using a symbol of life and what supports it, that is, by means of food and drink. This is represented by "bread and wine," as it were, archetypally prefigured when "King Melchizedek of Salem brought out bread and wine; he was priest of God Most High" (Gen 14:18).

St. Augustine offers the following explanation:

> Thus a true sacrifice is every work which is done that we may be united to God in holy fellowship, and which has a reference to that supreme good and end in which alone we can be truly blessed. And therefore even the mercy we show to men, if it is not shown for God's sake, is not a sacrifice. For, though made or offered by man, sacrifice is a divine thing, as those who called it *sacrifice* meant to indicate. Thus man himself, consecrated in the name of God, and vowed to God, is a sacrifice in so far as he dies to the world that he may live to God. (*Civ.* X,6)

Tradition had always seen in the sacrifice of Melchizedek (Gen 14:18) the model for the eucharistic sacrifice, which is offered with bread and wine in thanksgiving to the Creator of heaven and earth and from which Abraham obtains blessing and salvation. Thus the Council of Trent's teaching on the sacrifice of the Mass begins: "As the apostle testifies, there was no perfection under the former covenant because of the insufficiency of the levitical priesthood. It was, therefore, necessary (according to the merciful ordination of God the Father) that another priest arise 'according to the order of Melchizedek,' our Lord Jesus Christ, who could make perfect all who were to be sanctified and bring them to fulfillment" (DH 1739).

ANALOGOUS TERMINOLOGICAL USAGE AND SETTING THE ECUMENICAL COURSE

Merely looking at the still fluid terminology used in the first two centuries to refer to offices actually distracts us from grasping their content, that is, the Christological foundation of the office of the apostles, the early Christian missionaries, the bishops and presbyters as pastors and leaders of the liturgical worship of God in the sacraments. Such an approach can lead to the systematic fallacy that so-called profane official titles are evidence of a profane understanding of office in biblical times and early Christianity, which was then influenced by the pagan sacred sacrificial cult and the sacred cultic ministry (of the priests) belonging to it, so that it became more and more alienated from itself with sacral categories of paganism. Incidentally, in the Germanic and Romance languages, the loan word "priest" and its variants come from "presbyter." As a result of comparisons made in the history of religion, the Christian concepts of presbyters as priests also came to be applied to ministers of pagan cults outside Graeco-Roman culture. This foreign infiltration of the Christian bishop and presbyter by the priest-*sacerdos* concept in the course of religious history paradoxically made it possible to state that, even though the term *priest* is derived from *presbyter*, there were no priests in the New Testament. Incredible though it may sound, the Catholic-Reformed controversy begins with a confusion of terminology. The formal translation of *hiereus/sacerdos* into German *Priester* and its equivalents in other languages (all of which come from the biblical "presbyter") contributed to immense confusion as to the definition of the content of these terms. The concept of *sacerdos/*priest must be applied analogously to Christ, the apostles, bishops, presbyters, and the common priesthood of all the faithful, not univocally or even equivocally. This would put the question of the religious office on the right track towards a final understanding.

It is crucial in the confusion of the history of the terms and the varying use of the same ones for different contents to take a look at the matter itself.

Christ made people from among his circle of disciples partakers of his consecration and mission. He appointed them ministers of his word and shepherds of his flock. Paul, as an apostle of Jesus Christ called directly by the Lord, had conferred on him, together with his brother Timothy, the "ministry of reconciliation" (2 Cor 5:18). That is the biblical foundation for the religious office as a continuation of apostolic ministry:

> [I]n Christ God was reconciling the world to himself, not counting their trespasses against them, and entrusting the message of reconciliation to us. So we are ambassadors for Christ, since God is making his appeal through us; we entreat you on behalf of Christ, be reconciled to God. (2 Cor 5:19f.)

This, in the soteriological sense, priestly dimension of the apostles' ministry is also expressed in Paul's great portrayal of the event of salvation in his Letter to the Romans: "[O]n some points I have written to you rather boldly by way of reminder, because of the grace given me by God to be a minister of Christ Jesus to the Gentiles in the priestly service of the gospel of God, so that the offering of the Gentiles may be acceptable, sanctified by the Holy Spirit" (Rom 15:15f.).

Corresponding to the reference backwards in creation theology is the messianic-eschatological promise of the pure sacrifice that will be offered to God's name in every place to make his name great among the nations (cf. Mal 1:11) and to proclaim it.

In the eschatological time of salvation, the beginning is taken up again and brought to its completion. Christ has the messianic priesthood according to the order of Melchizedek (Ps 110:4; Heb 7:17).

However comparative religion might define the sacrifice in form and content, what counts for Christianity is its real definition, the one that comes from Christianity's understanding of the relationship between God and the world in creation and its reading of history based on sin and redemption. This holds true for Christ's sacrifice on the Cross and for the making present of it in the Mass as the sacrifice of Christ and the Church.

THE INSTRUMENTAL CAUSALITY OF THE SACRAMENTS

In the series of causes, the sacraments are important for justification as instrumental causes. As the glory of God is the final cause, God's mercy the efficient cause, and Christ's redemptive sacrifice the meritorious cause of the justification, forgiveness, and sanctification (divinization) of the sinner, so the sacraments are, as it were, instruments through which the grace is applied to human beings. They are efficacious signs and means of grace. As far as the formal cause is concerned, there is complete agreement with Luther's concerns. For it is the justice of God with which he justifies us out of pure grace (*iustitia Dei passiva*) and not the justice in which he is in himself just and punishes our sins (*iustitia Dei activa*) that is the formal, that is, defining, cause of our being "called children of God; and that is what we are" (1 Jn 3:1). In contrast to Luther, Catholic doctrine teaches that righteousness of faith is not mediated to us by faith alone (*sola fide qua fiducia*), but through "faith formed by love" (*fides caritate formata*) (cf. Gal 5:6).

So the general concept of the sacrament and the understanding of Christ's human nature as the organ of his divine salvific will both mark a distinction between the Catholic view of the sacramental priesthood and the Protestant office of preacher and pastor.

Canon 8 of the Decree on the Sacraments (3 March 1547) states clearly: "If anyone says that through the sacraments of the New Law grace is not conferred by the performance of the rite itself (*ex opere operato*) but that faith alone in the divine promise is sufficient to obtain grace, let him be anathema" (DH 1608).

Applied to the priesthood, it can be concluded that sacred ordination (*sacra ordinatio*) is truly and properly a sacrament instituted by Christ. It is considerably more than just a rite by which ministers of the word and sacraments are chosen (DH 1773).

"If anyone says that by sacred ordination the Holy Spirit is not given and that, therefore, the bishops say in vain: 'Receive the Holy Spirit'; or if he says that no character is imprinted by ordination; or that he who has once been a priest can again become a layman, let him be anathema" (DH 1774).

THE OBJECTIVE
EFFICACY OF THE SACRAMENTS

The tension between the historical uniqueness of the sacrifice of the Cross and the daily celebration of this sacrifice in the Mass cannot be surmounted via the subjective memory of the faithful but only through the objectivity of the sacrament that Christ instituted at the Last Supper with the commission to celebrate this rite in his memory, so as to participate in his Cross and his Resurrection. Since Luther commented on Peter Lombard's *Book of Sentences* in his lectures, he must have been familiar with the following passage, which should have dispelled his doubts as to the sacrificial character of the Mass: the sacrifice of the Mass is offered because it "*memoria est et repræsentatio sacrificii veri et sanctæ immolationis facta in ara crucis. Et semel Christus mortuus est, in cruce scilicet,—ibique immolatus est in semetipso; quotidie autem immolatur in sacramento, quia in sacramento recordatio fit illius quod factum est semel*" (*Sent.* IV, dist. XII, cap.5). Luther had also studied the extensive explanation of the Mass by Gabriel Biel (1415–1495), "the last scholastic," which in fact reduces the criticism Luther levels at priests and the sacrifice of the Mass to nothing. Only with the help of a sacramental way of thinking that is nonetheless really rooted in the Incarnation can the relationship between the sacrifice of the Cross and the sacrifice of the Mass be correctly expressed.

DIFFERENCES IN ANTHROPOLOGY

Neither in a Lutheran religious nor in a Kantian transcendental-philosophical way can the human person be divided, as it were dualistically, into an empirical self and a transcendental self. Then, only grace would give the person his or her identity before God. Man's person is a substance of soul and body united in itself, for *omne ens est unum*. This has nothing to do with substance metaphysics versus the philosophy of the person as relation because man is by virtue of having been created already inalienably a person in relation to God and to other people. Man does not lose his personhood through sin, but only the possibility of its supreme perfection in the divine virtues of faith, hope, and love. It cannot be that a baptized person experiences himself empirically as a sinner, an enemy of God, and a hater of God, and yet believes himself transcendentally, through the assurance of Christ's righteousness, to be a friend of God who must for this reason—in a faith that is constantly re-confirming itself— suppress nature, rebelling against God in its physical drives and mental appetites. Because of the substantial unity of man in his spiritual-physical nature, there can be no separation of the empirical self and the transcendental self. In modern times, the speculative contrast between Catholic and Protestant theology and between the ontological and the transcendental approach in philosophy has its beginnings in the concept of *natura totaliter corrupta*. The human striving for self-preservation and increasing one's possibilities can be perverted into egoism, but it is not per se and of necessity bad. For this reason, the world, culture, and the state are also not realities that are completely neutral with respect to salvation (*heilsneutral*) and have to be dealt with in a pragmatic and utilitarian way. Nature and grace, science and faith, moral endeavor and the gratuity of grace, responsibility for the world and love of God over everything, earth and heaven—these are all to be distinguished, but not separated from one another. Man's physical and mental abilities to strive are not in themselves bad because they, too, are embraced by his nature of being made in the image of God, which cannot be destroyed even by sin.

The speculative idea of the Protestant doctrine of justification has its roots in the failure to distinguish between the finite per se and evil as the negation of the will of God. This then leads to a rejection of the merit of good works, the unconditional validity of natural moral law, the objective efficacy of the sacraments, the sacramental priesthood and holy Mass, and the authority of the pope and the council by divine law. In the Protestant view, the consciousness of being a creature and hence not God is always combined with some sort of feeling of sinfulness. The creature cannot bear not being God and "will be like God" (Gen 3:5). There is always a certain rebellion against God, even in "religion as a feeling of absolute dependence" on the Absolute, that is, God (Schleiermacher), or in the identity of identity and nonidentity (Hegel).

It is different in the underlying eucharistic feeling of owing oneself totally to one's heavenly Father in his Son and of being loved in the Spirit of both from all eternity and of loving God eternally. The dialectic of *simul iustus et peccator* can only be escaped, against all experience of being a sinner, if it becomes a consoling certainty to me (transcendentally) in faith that I am one with God.[10]

Against this it must, however, be stated that man experiences himself as, and knows himself to be, an original union of body and soul. Therefore the first act of self-reflection is to see the unity—instead of the splitness—of the person and the dialectical disunity between the interior and the exterior perspective, between subject and object, world and self. The naturally good and the free will cannot be removed at all because they are identical with the will of the Creator, through whom every human being exists.

With respect to the conjugal community of man and woman and hence the understanding of the sacramentality of marriage (which Luther denies), it is necessary to grasp the dynamic and integrative unity of *sexus*, eros, and agape resulting from the unity of nature and grace. The counter model to this would be the idea that the baser, egoistic urges had to be tamed by grace or that nature should be given free rein by freeing it from being alienated from itself by culture (Rousseau).

Perception of the unity and differentiation of nature and grace is also the prerequisite for a correct understanding of the soteriological dogma. It makes it possible to see the objective reality of the sacraments. Even Christologically one cannot maintain that through the holy exchange the human substance of Christ had become sin and Jesus himself had become the greatest of criminals while we as the committers of mortal sin participate in his divine substance. The communication of properties (or idioms) that Luther appealed to signifies an exchange of human and divine attributes that applies to the divine person of the Logos, not his two natures.

Due to the unity of the divine and human natures in the person of the Son of the Father, the opposition between a gift of God to us (katabatic line) and man's sacrifice for God (anabatic line) is removed, or rather the two are combined into one. On the Cross and in the Mass, Christ is the same sacrificial offering and the same sacrificial priest in one. He is simultaneously God's gift to us in his humanity and, as the head of humankind, vicariously our total gift of ourselves to God. Through

Christ's bearing our sins as the Lamb of God and, on the altar of the Cross, wiping out our punishment, destroying death and God-forsakenness in the ocean of the Father's love, his Resurrection becomes for us the gate through which we enter into community with the triune God. Through, with, and in Christ we give thanks to the Father and glorify in the Holy Spirit God our Creator, Redeemer, and Perfecter.

On account of his doctrine of man's total depravity in Adam's sin, Luther was bound to view every sacrifice by man as self-justification. Even though the sacrifices of pagans were often perverted in their object and means by sin, there is a primal anthropological truth that nevertheless emerges from behind all the depravity: man is a creature who wishes to express his thanks for being created and hence his thanks to the Creator of the world and of mankind. Christ thus cancels out the imperfection of pagan and Jewish sacrifices and their priests. But as the Son of God who offers himself as an oblation to the Father in carrying out the plan of salvation, he absorbs into himself the intentions of all sacrifices hitherto offered by mankind, and especially those of the People of God in the Mosaic covenant. He unites mankind in himself, and on the Cross, in the unity of the sacrificial priest and sacrificial offering of his obedience, offers himself to God, his Father. Therein lies the new and eternal covenant, which is represented as a symbolic reality, that is, sacramentally, in every celebration commemorating his one unique propitiatory sacrifice.

THE INCARNATION AS FACT AND AS A PRINCIPLE OF FAITH

In the person-creating procession of the divine person of the Son from the Father and their relationship with one another the Son is already Eucharist in person. He owes himself eternally to the Father's communication of his divinity. Through the Incarnation he is the Immanuel—God with us. And as a human being he embodies man's radical relatedness to the triune God as God's children and friends. When he institutes the everlasting memorial of his Passion at the Last Supper, Jesus takes the bread and wine into his hands. These are the gifts of God through which we as his creatures are sustained, strengthened, and filled with a zest for life. In his hands he connects these gifts with his body and his human nature and turns them into symbols of his gratitude to the Creator. The Son gives thanks to the Father for the creation and preservation of mankind.

CHRIST IS EUCHARIST IN PERSON

We are included in Jesus' thanksgiving for eternally receiving his divinity from the Father and temporarily receiving his human nature. In this he is the head of mankind, and his disciples are united in him into his Body, the Church. But the Son of God is also sent by the Father "in the likeness of sinful flesh, and to deal with sin, he condemned sin in the flesh, so that the just requirement of the law might be fulfilled in us, who walk not according to the flesh but according to the Spirit" (Rom 8:3f.). Therefore the death that Jesus suffers vicariously for our sins also signifies reconciliation with God and renewal of the covenant with God: "This cup is the new covenant in my blood. Do this, as often as you drink it, in remembrance of me. For as often as you eat this bread and drink the cup, you proclaim the Lord's death until he comes" (1 Cor 11:25f.).

"The cup of blessing that we bless, is it not a sharing in the blood of Christ?" says the apostle (1 Cor 10:16), as God's gift to us and as our giving of ourselves to him and thus the sacrifice of the whole Body of Christ, of the head of its members. Because of this, the eucharistic sacrifice of the Church is the highest form of the worship, adoration, and glorification of God, for we offer him not something material but rather, in Christ, present our bodies "as a living sacrifice, holy and acceptable to God, which is your spiritual worship" (Rom 12:1). It is the Christians' true worship of God, in accordance with the Logos Christ, that we, through him, "continually offer a sacrifice of praise to God, that is, the fruit of lips that confess his name" (Heb 13:15) and show mercy and justice towards our neighbor for the love of Christ. As Christ on the Cross brought about once and for all the renewal and perpetuation of God's covenant with his eschatological People of God, made up of Jews and Gentiles (cf. Eph 2:14), with his Blood in expiation for our sins, so holy Mass is in itself the making present of the one unique sacrifice of Christ in all its constitutive elements. It is praise, worship, and glorification of God. It is a sacrifice of thanksgiving and petition for ourselves and for others. It is a propitiatory sacrifice offered for all the sins of mankind, including my own that I have committed in my personal life (Trent, *Decretum de sacrificio missae*, can 3: DH 1753).

For in each of the many liturgical celebrations that we perform in commemoration of Christ's one historical sacrifice on the Cross, "you proclaim the Lord's death until he comes" (1 Cor 11:26). Christ allows us to partake in his Blood of the new covenant (cf. 1 Cor 10:16; 1 Cor 11:25) "that is poured out for you" (Lk 22:20), "poured out for many for the forgiveness of sins" (Mt 26:28; cf. Mk 14:24). There is not in any way a change of subject from the sacrifice of the Cross to the sacrifice of the Mass, with Christ offering himself to the Father in the former and the priest offering Christ as the oblation at Mass. For in both priest and oblation are the same Christ who offers himself to the Father for the salvation of the world. The priest merely acts liturgically and spiritually in the person of Christ. He at the same time offers himself and the whole Church in Christ. Inasmuch as Christ on the Cross offered himself to the Father in heaven in his natural body and in the sacrifice of the Mass he now does so in his sacramental and ecclesial body. "*Una enim eademque est hostia, idem nunc offerens sacerdotum ministerio, qui se ipsum in cruce obtulit, sola offerendi ratione diversa*" (DH 1743).

The criticism the prophets (Hos 6:6) and Jesus (Mt 9:13) directed against an externalized, reified sacrifice without mercy and love of neighbor does not apply to the eucharistic sacrifice instituted by Christ himself, which in fact overcomes such a sacrifice: "But when Christ came as a high priest of the good things that have come, then through the greater and perfect tent (not made with hands, that is, not of this creation), he entered once for all into the Holy Place, not with the blood of goats and calves, but with his own blood, thus obtaining eternal redemption" (Heb 9:11f.).

However, this criticism remains a lasting warning to the conscience of every Christian not to sever liturgy from *diakonia*, worship of God in the sacramental commemoration of Jesus from discipleship of him in active love of neighbor. Christianity is not a this-worldly humanistic ethic but rather "that you may proclaim the mighty acts" (1 Pt 2:9) of God and worship his might and glory.

COMMUNION OF THE DIVINE LIFE IN CHRIST

The recent discussion within Catholicism as to whether the Mass is a sacrifice *or* a meal basically misses the essence of holy Mass with this pseudo-alternative. Likewise those efforts to try to reduce the one aspect to the other or deduce one from the other fail to take into account the reality of faith. For the Mass is not a religious commemorative meal for a long-since-deceased person, but rather the making present of Christ's sacrifice on the Cross through which we achieve reconciliation with God and *thereby* communion with the Father and the Son in the Holy Spirit.

In Canon 1 of the Decree on the Most Holy Sacrifice of the Mass (1563), the Council of Trent anathematizes anyone who says "that in the Mass a true and proper sacrifice is not offered to God or that the offering consists merely in the fact that Christ is given to us to eat" (DH 1751). This community of life is granted us as a reality when we consume the sacramental Body and Blood of Christ. Only those who offer themselves in love and with their whole being and life to God the Father through and in Christ have community of life with him, the risen Lord. "Whoever eats of this bread will live for ever; and the bread that I will give for the life of the world is my flesh" (Jn 6:51). The Eucharist is the sacrament in which the one unique sacrifice of Christ on the Cross becomes really present *in symbolo*, so that the faithful participating at the Mass give themselves to the Father in Christ. In the obedience of faith and the fire of love they become spiritually one with his Son. Through eating the sacramental flesh of Christ and drinking his blood under the species of wine they become spiritually one body with him (cf. 1 Cor 10:16f.) and they are "all made to drink of one Spirit" (1 Cor 12:13). Naturally we do not eat Christ's Body and drink his Blood in their own natural forms but rather in their sacramental forms, so that a spiritual community of life results. The life of the body is the soul, but the life of the soul is the grace of the *Verbum incarnatum*.

Scarcely anyone has expressed the connection between the sacrifice of mercy and the eucharistic sacrifice of Christ and the Church better than St. Augustine, the founding father of Luther's order:

> Since, therefore, true sacrifices are works of mercy to ourselves or others, done with a reference to God, [. . .] it follows that the whole redeemed city, that is to say, the congregation or community of the saints, is offered to God as our sacrifice through the great high priest, who offered Himself to God in His passion for us, that we might be members of this glorious head, according to the form of a servant. For it was this form He offered, in this He was offered, because it is according to it He is Mediator, in this He is our Priest, in this the Sacrifice.[. . .] This is the sacrifice of Christians: we, being many, are one body in Christ. And this also is the sacrifice which the Church continually celebrates in the sacrament of the altar, known to the faithful, in which she teaches that she herself is offered in the offering she makes to God. (*Civ.* X,6)

CHRIST IS THE SAME ON THE CROSS AND IN THE CELEBRATION OF THE EUCHARIST

Thus it is possible today, after the clarifications achieved in ecumenical dialogue, to state quite correctly that the sixteenth-century doctrinal condemnations do not apply to the self-understanding of our dialogue partner today. I do, however, believe that even before the disputes began from 1517 onwards and before the Council of Trent there was no contentual contradiction between the magisterium's understanding of the sacrifice of the Mass and the sacramental priesthood on the one hand and the Reformed and general Christian understanding of the "first and chief article," as Luther called the justification of the sinner through grace alone without performing works of the law in the *Smalcald Articles* (II,2).

Viewing the working of God's grace and its mediation through the sacraments as alternatives was only a seeming opposition.

Of course, the transformation of the substances of bread and wine into the substance of the Body and Blood of Christ is brought about solely through the working of the Holy Spirit in the power of Christ. However, that does not exclude all human causality; rather it includes *ratione sacramenti*, an instrumental causality of the human words of consecration spoken by the validly ordained priest. The spiritually fruitful effect depends on the faith and love of the recipient as long as there is no mortal sin impeding union with Christ (Thomas Aquinas, *S.th.* III q.79 a.3).

For the effect of a tool comes in different ways from both the tool and the craftsman. As a result of the Incarnation, man is not just the addressee of divine action. Through his human nature, which is united with his divine nature without confusion or separation, Jesus brings about salvation. His humanity serves his divinity as an organ and instrument of mediating salvation. Therefore at the Eucharist Christ is the real subject of the sacrifice to the Father and its being offered to us as the food of eternal life. But the priest—in the spiritual authority bestowed on him by Christ—speaks and acts in the liturgy by speaking the words of institution mandated by Christ as an instrumental cause.

The signs of the sacrament that are manifest to the senses and the celebrating priest do not themselves effect either the grace or the change of essence of the bread and wine into Christ's Body and Blood; rather, they bring this about as instruments of the divine and as representatives of Christ, the head of the Church.

This also counters the objection that it is not the pope who is head of the Church but Christ alone. Yes, Christ is indeed the sole head of the Church. But for the universal Church the visible representative of Christ is the pope; for the particular church it is the bishop; and for the congregation assembled at Mass it is the priest. Through each of these the Lord himself proclaims the unity of all Christians. With respect to the divine-human reality of the Church, which has its roots in the mystery of the Incarnation, Johann Adam Möhler says: "The Church, his permanent manifestation, is at once divine and human; she is the union of both. He it is who, concealed under earthly and human forms, works in the Church. [. . .] Hence these two parts change their predicates. If the divine, the living Christ and his spirit constitute undoubtedly that which is infallible, and eternally inerrable in the Church; so also the human is infallible and inerrable in the same way, because the divine without the human has no existence for us: yet the human is not inerrable in itself, but only as the organ, and as the manifestation of the divine."[11]

St. Augustine already asks how it fits together that Christ is the one shepherd and yet many people as members of his Body visibly represent him as its head (cf. *Tr. in Io.* 46). Christ as the head is the sole author of grace, which passes from him to all the members of his Body. But as a visible society the Church needs people who, by virtue of their ordination and task, embody her visible unity. "First, inasmuch as Christ is the Head of all who pertain to the Church in every place and time and state; but all other men are called heads with reference to certain special places, as bishops of their Churches. Or with reference to a determined time as the Pope is the head of the whole Church, viz. during the time of his Pontificate, and with reference to a determined state, inasmuch as they are in the state of wayfarers. Secondly, because Christ is the Head of the Church by His own power and authority; while others are called heads, as taking Christ's place" (Thomas Aquinas, *S.th.* III q.8 a.6).

6.

THE ORIGIN OF THE PRIESTHOOD IN JESUS' MESSIANIC AUTHORITY AND MISSION

Dear Confreres and Friends,

During my studies from the 1967–68 academic year onwards, the New Testament professor shocked us by stating that there was no biblical foundation for the Catholic priesthood to which we were striving to dedicate our lives. For many, this pulled the rug out from under their feet. The failure of many a priestly calling and vocation was not due solely to the conflict between celibacy and the sexual revolution of the 1968 generation; it was in fact to an ever greater extent the result of the dogmatic foundations beginning to totter. It is wrong to blame the Second Vatican Council for the crisis in the period that followed it and the failure of many vocations. The seeming absence of any basis for the Catholic priesthood in what Christ intended to found has contributed greatly to the identity crisis of priests as far as dogmatics, morality, and pastoral care are concerned. This even shows itself in their outward appearance. Some are no longer to be recognized by their clerical dress but rather by their markedly tasteless clothes and poor social skills. If you separate priestly functions from a worldly private life, you have already failed to fulfill the essence and mission of the priest.

Since grace presupposes, exalts, and perfects nature, precisely the sacred ministry, which places the highest of all demands on its bearers, also requires a good natural foundation: a well-formed human character, a comprehensive intellectual education, and a nobleness of heart, loving God with all one's heart and with all one's might, and loving one's neighbor as oneself.

Even though it is objectively false, it has been and still is contended in progressive and liberal writings that there is no Christological foundation for the ordained priesthood. Jesus, so the anachronistic argument goes, was a "layman" since he did not belong to the Levitical priesthood of the sacrificial cult of the Temple. The offices, they maintain, came about in accordance with sociological criteria and resulted from the needs of the respective communities and circumstances. The New Testament is not regarded as testifying to the faith of the Church that was taking shape from Jesus via the apostles down to the latter's disciples; rather they regard it as a loose collection of diverse intellectual and social constructs in which more or less anonymous "communities" put together their impressions of "Jesus." This would then mean that the apostles' testimony to Christ's Incarnation and Resurrection contained nothing more than interpretative tools and not accounts of facts. In the opinion of David Friedrich Strauss (1808–1874), the gospels are nothing more than *"geschichtsartige Einkleidungen urchristlicher Ideen, gebildet in der absichtslos dichten Sage"* (primitive Christian ideas clothed in what looks like history, framed in the undesignedly compact legend).[12]

In negating the truth that is supported by existence and historical facts, the hermeneutics of Enlightenment rationalism—as well as of empiricism and positivism—regards the gospels as mere myths and theologoumena, that is, theological *"Begriffs-dichtung"* (conceptual poetry). If the Church's Creed were merely a montage of feelings and ideas that an individual or collective subject takes turns in putting together in various cultures, then faith, too, can be de-composed again or re-composed in a different key. The principles of deconstructionism are, however, by no means obvious; rather, they are self-contradictory. The historical-critical method in the interpretation of sacred scripture and the history of dogma does not in itself undermine the faith of the Church but only when it uncritically adopts the premises of empirical positivism.

But since God reveals himself in his word and through the medium of human language and makes his salvific will known in historical events, dogmatic synthesis and historical analysis form one substantial unity. They do not stand in opposition to one another like immediate and un-mediateable approaches of quite different natures. The very fact of the Incarnation, with its unity of word and event, means that historicity as a condition for cognizing the truths of reason and revelation does not constitute the triumph of relativism but rather the definitive overcoming of it. In his infinite-finite spiritual nature, man is a hearer of a potential word of God expressed in human language and understood through concepts and ideas, that is, understood in its character as an assertion of truth.

To the Word that has become flesh and communicates with them in their language Peter says, together with the twelve apostles, that is, the representatives of the Church: "You have the words of eternal life" (Jn 6:68). Jesus is in his person at one and the same time "the way" (hermeneutics) and "the truth" (knowledge) and "the life" (fellowship with the Father). The faith of the Church rests on the reality of historical revelation. It is not a subject-immanent feeling of internal and external religious impulses. If the apostles had not been "eyewitnesses and servants of the word" (Lk 1:2) but merely interpreters of their individual or collective religious sentiments, that would leave us with no more than a functional understanding of the priestly office. Instead of being servants and witnesses of the word who "walk in the truth" (3 Jn 1:3), bishops and priests would then have to offer their work for sale on the market of religions and ideologies, gurus, meaning-givers, providers of rites, and organizers of humanitarian aid—naturally for a fee. But the apostles' service of salvation is not a trading of God's grace; otherwise

grace would not be grace. When he commissioned and sent out
the apostles, Jesus said: "You received without payment; give
without payment" (Mt 10:8). If one were to cast fundamental
doubt on the ontological and historical reality of revelation,
there could be no question of the apostolic office's having been
divinely instituted, apart from the vague working of a "divine"
spirit, which, however, anyone can lay claim to for his or her
own ideas and ambitions. Such an office would also not have
the spiritual authority to sanctify the people and lead them as
their shepherds to eternal life in the power of Christ's Spirit. It
would amount to nothing more than taking care of the external
organization of a club of like-minded people and indoctrinating
them with one's own ideology.

At the end of the great discourse at the sending out of the
Twelve, Jesus explains the origin of the sacramental office as
lying in his own sending by the Father, a mission in which the
apostles and their successors participate in the offices of bishops
and priests: "Whoever welcomes you welcomes me, and whoever
welcomes me welcomes the one who sent me" (Mt 10:40).

A DEEPER UNDERSTANDING:
PAUL AND THE LETTER
TO THE HEBREWS

By contrast, the salvific effect of the Redemption through the
sacrifice of the Cross, which in the Letter to the Hebrews is
interpreted using the category of a completely unique high
priesthood according to the order of Melchizedek, depends on
his being the Son of God. Herein lies the radical difference:
the Church is either a supernaturally founded real fellowship
(*koinonia*) with God which mediates grace or it is a gathering of
those who take their spiritual and moral bearings from a religious founding figure and his descendants which was founded
and is led by human beings.

Even though the service of the apostles as pastors and teachers is not fully captured by the terms *hiereus* and the corresponding Latin *sacerdos*, this does not prevent us from making the objective statement that the apostles, in the name and authority of Christ, the universal Redeemer and High Priest and Mediator of the new covenant, continued Christ's salvific mission from the Father by making it present through word and sacrament. The Letter to the Hebrews interprets the whole of Christ's work of salvation through the category of the priesthood according to Melchizedek and sees in Christ the one and only mediator of the new and eternal covenant. Yet the letter does not rule out the exercise of Christ's salvific ministry by the apostles and the overseers of the Church; in fact it includes this. For the author of Hebrews the title "high priest" as a soteriological category is a synonym for "our Lord Jesus, the great shepherd of the sheep" (Heb 13:20). The same is expressed in the image of the "good shepherd" who lays down his life for the sheep of God's flock (cf. Jn 10:11).

And Jesus made his apostles and *episkopoi* and presbyters into shepherds who feed his sheep in his name. When people maintain that the Letter to the Hebrews excludes the priestly ministry of the pastors of the Church or that in the First Letter of Peter the official priesthood has been absorbed into the universal priesthood of the community, this is nothing more than terminological equivocation: there is no *fundamentum in re* to support an objective rejection of the sanctifying, that is, priestly, ministry of the shepherds in the episcopate and presbyterate.

And even if the terms for the subsequent offices of *episkopoi* and presbyters did come from the secular rather than the cultic sphere, this in no way speaks against their purpose being to lead God's Church in Christ's name and to translate Christ's salvation efficaciously into the life of the faithful in the form of signs. After all, the polytheistic and pantheistic division of the world into a profane and a sacred sphere plays no role whatsoever in the context of biblical belief in God. Rather, the whole world is related to holy God in creation and covenant, in redemption and justification. The Church is neither spatially nor ethically separated from the world, but in it; and for the world she is "in Christ like a sacrament or as a sign and instrument both of a very closely knit union with God and of the unity of the whole human race" (*LG* 1). She performs her service of proclaiming the gospel of reconciliation in her basic tasks of *martyria, leiturgia,* and *diakonia.*

The sacred place in Christian liturgy is not the demarcated area for the numinosum of a deity. The temple, house, and sanctuary of God is the sacred gathering of the faithful, in which Christ sanctifies the people through the sacraments, which consist of natural symbols and human words, and offers them to the Father as the fruit of the Redemption brought about by him. The priest is the servant of Jesus Christ in his word and the sacred symbols of the liturgy and not the servant of a deity to whom he has to offer sacrifices in order to appease the blind forces of fate in nature and history. If the bishops and then also the presbyters are first referred to in Greek as *hiereus* and in Latin as *sacerdos* (and the bishop as chief pastor also as *summus sacerdos*), this merely expresses the Christological foundation of the spiritual office and has nothing whatsoever to do with a reversion to the sacrificial cult for pagan deities. The Christian Creed did not come into being subsequent to studying the writings of early Christian communities but actually precedes the writings of the New Testament. It is therefore not a construct of confused feelings and foggy thinking projected back into the historical life of Jesus, about which we know relatively little, but rather the result of knowledge of the revealed truth.

THE ORIGINAL TESTIMONY: SACRED SCRIPTURE

The apostles were witnesses to the event of God's self-revelation in Jesus, to his person, his surrendering himself to the Father and to the acceptance of the Son by the Father, that is, the justification of the Crucified Son by raising him from the dead through the Holy Spirit. The teaching of the apostles, from which the baptismal profession of faith was formed, is the product and resonance chamber of the self-revelation of the eternal Son of the Father. That is why the four canonical gospels are not a conglomerate of sayings and stories about Jesus. They are held together like the members of a body by the soul as their vital and organizing principle. This is the unity of Father and Son that is revealed in the Holy Spirit. Jesus said: "All things have been handed over to me by my Father; and no one knows who the Son is except the Father, or who the Father is except the Son and anyone to whom the Son chooses to reveal him" (Lk 10:22; cf. Mt 11:25ff.).

After rising from the dead and before being seated at the right hand of the Father to exercise his rule in the new kingdom of God, Jesus charges the eleven disciples with a universal mission because now all authority in heaven and on earth has been given to him.

> All authority in heaven and on earth has been given to me. Go therefore and make disciples of all nations, baptizing them in the name of the Father and of the Son and of the Holy Spirit, and teaching them to obey everything that I have commanded you. And remember, I am with you always, to the end of the age.
>
> —Matthew 28:18–20

This says everything about the legitimacy of the Church and of the apostolic office of the apostles and their successors, who come to be called bishops and presbyters (that is, priests). They exercise their ministry for the building up of the Church and the growth of the Body of Christ by being teachers and pastors to the faithful, those sanctified in Christ and the Holy Spirit (cf. Eph 4:11).

In their finally edited form (ca. AD 70–90), the gospels are likely to have been completed in the period between AD 40 and

AD 50, that is, later than the epistles of the apostle Paul, which give us insights into the creed and life of his communities just a few years after his conversion. In his double-work of Luke-Acts, the evangelist interlocks Jesus' historical self-revelation with his living presence in the post-Easter Church of the Holy Spirit. And at the same time he links the sending out of Jesus' disciples with Paul at their head with the mission of Paul, the apostle to the Gentiles, which leads into the center of the ecumene, the inhabited world. In Rome, Paul was "proclaiming the kingdom of God and teaching about the Lord Jesus Christ with all boldness and without hindrance" (Acts 28:31).

But because the Holy Roman Church owes her apostolic foundation and her constitution to "the two most glorious apostles," she is also in the succession of her bishops and her Creed the most important guarantor of the true and entire tradition of the teaching of the apostles and the word of God. "For it is a matter of necessity that every Church should agree with this Church, on account of its preeminent authority" (*Haer.* 3,3,2), Irenaeus declared in the second half of the second century.

But with the echoes of the original testimony of Jesus' disciples to be found in the history of the impact of the churches these disciples founded, the gospels portray the *primitive* and *supernatural* faith of the early Church. They were never intended to be just historical testimonies of empirically identifiable events; rather, their purpose was to bear unique, constitutive, and lasting witness to the mystery of the person of Jesus in his relationship to God. Hence the biblical witness can never be merely the starting point for an ascent to a summit where systematic theology, liberated from the ballast of positive theology, can rejoice in its speculations.

The word of God in sacred scripture is the ever-bubbling fountain that refreshes and invigorates us with the living water of the presence of Christ. And all the fruits of the faith grown from the matrix of the apostolic and ecclesial tradition are fed from the fount that is the living Christ himself. He speaks the "words of eternal life" (Jn 6:68) that proceed from the one Word

of God that "was with God, and . . . was God" (Jn 1:1): "He is
the true God and eternal life" (1 Jn 5:20).

For an understanding of the origin of the Catholic priesthood and the form it took on, and of its essence and shape, we
need to follow three methodological steps:

1. The question of its origin in Jesus' being sent by the Father
2. The question of the understanding of apostolic ministry and
   its spirituality in Paul
3. The question of the normative form the office of bishops and
   presbyters had taken on by the transition from its apostolic
   foundations to the capturing of its essence in the Creed and
   in the liturgy of the Church

THE ENDURING ORIGIN OF ALL MISSION IN JESUS CHRIST, THE SON OF THE FATHER

"And the Word became flesh and lived among us, and we have
seen his glory, the glory as of a father's only son, full of grace
and truth" (Jn 1:14).

Trinity and Incarnation are the primal ground and formal
ground of the apostolate. The risen Lord appears to his disciples
and shares with them the paschal peace, the life-giving gift of
his fellowship with the Father in the Holy Spirit. The Son gives
them a share in his mission and confers on them the life-breath
of the Holy Spirit.

> "As the Father has sent me, so I send you." When he
> had said this, he breathed on them and said to them,
> "Receive the Holy Spirit. If you forgive the sins of
> any, they are forgiven them; if you retain the sins of
> any, they are retained."
>
> —John 20:21–23

The authority and mission from the Father are conferred on the *episkopoi*/presbyters in the Holy Spirit by the exalted Lord (Acts 20:28). Timothy, the "co-worker for God in proclaiming the gospel of Christ" (1 Thess 3:2) and fellow apostle of St. Paul, is already consecrated in the apostolic succession in order to preserve the precious good of the faith and to entrust it "to faithful people who will be able to teach others as well" (2 Tim 2:2). These are the *episkopoi*/presbyters together with the deacons (Phil 1:1; 1 Tim 3:1–13; Ti 1:5–9) about whom we hear in Acts and the Letters to Timothy and Titus, and who are the prototypes of the successors of the apostles.

The principle of the succession is clearly in evidence even though it is not theologically developed until St. Irenaeus of Lyon's battle against Gnosticism 80–100 years later. At about the same time as the letters to the pastors Timothy and Titus, which contain Paul's legacy to the Church after his death, the Roman Church issues a clear dogmatic statement to the Corinthians, who have deposed their legitimate bishops/presbyters, basing it on the words of Jesus when he sent out the apostles: "The apostles have preached the gospel to us from the Lord Jesus Christ; Jesus Christ [has done so] from God. Christ therefore was sent forth by God, and the apostles by Christ. Both these appointments, then, were made in an orderly way, according to the will of God" (*1 Clem* 42,1).

In their ministry they are all to recall Paul's admonition to Timothy: "to rekindle the gift of God that is within you through the laying on of my hands" (2 Tim 1:6; cf. 1 Tim 4:14; Acts 6:6, 14:23).

The content of the Sacrament of Holy Orders (*res sacramenti*) comes from Christ and consists in the conferral of Spirit and authority so as to be able to fulfill the mission of preaching, governing, and sanctifying in a spiritually effective way. The sacramental sign (*sacramentum tantum*) has since apostolic times consisted in the consecratory prayer and the laying on of hands, first by the apostles and then by the bishops, who possess the fullness of the Sacrament of Holy Orders. Timothy must be extremely careful in his selection of priests to be ordained. He is the supervisor of the presbyters: "I warn you to keep these instructions without prejudice, doing nothing on the basis of partiality. Do not lay hands on anyone hastily, and do not participate in the sins of others" (1 Tim 5:21f.).

THE KINGDOM OF GOD IS REALIZED IN THE LIFE AND WORK OF JESUS

As presented in the synoptic gospels, the mystery of Jesus' person and his mission from the Father is revealed in the story of his earthly life up to the Passion and Resurrection. He is "the Son of God" (Mk 1:1), "a ruler who is to shepherd my people Israel" (Mt 2:6), as God has promised. In proclaiming the gospel, he turns God's rule and kingdom into a reality. And he reveals his oneness with the Father through the fullness of his divine authority (cf. Mk 1:22; Mt 28:18) to heal the sick, comfort the suffering, gather in once more the scattered children of Israel, and inaugurate the year of the Lord's favor that would nevermore end (cf. Lk 4:19).

"Then Jesus went about all the cities and villages, teaching in their synagogues, and proclaiming the good news of the *kingdom* [*basileia*], and curing every disease and every sickness. When he saw the crowds, he had *compassion* for them, because they were harassed and helpless, like sheep without a shepherd" (Mt 9:35f., italics mine). In his divine and human compassion for us the Lord appoints coworkers in his pastoral ministry: "Then he said to his disciples, 'The harvest is plentiful, but the labourers are few; therefore ask the Lord of the harvest to send out labourers into his harvest'" (Mt 9:37f.).

So he takes a number of his disciples into the service of spreading the kingdom by instituting the Twelve as a firm circle of his apostles, coworkers in the Lord's vineyard, and fishers of people (cf. Mk 1:17).

> He [Jesus] went up the mountain and *called* to him
> those whom he *wanted*, and they *came* to him. And he
> *appointed twelve*, whom he also named apostles, to be
> *with him*, and to be *sent out* to *proclaim* the message, and
> to have *authority* to cast out demons.
> —Mark 3:13–15, italics mine

All the elements that are constitutive for the Catholic priesthood
are mentioned in the apostolate of the Twelve. Above all, the
constitution of the Church is not a structure with interchangeable functionaries but rather a relationship to Christ. He, the
Son of God anointed with the Holy Spirit, who took on our
human nature, was sent by the Father for the salvation of all
mankind. This Messiah of Israel, "who is called Christ" (Jn
4:25), is then recognized by Samaritans and Gentiles, too, as
"the Saviour of the world" (Jn 4:42). By virtue of his human
nature, which is anointed by the Holy Spirit, the eternal Son of
God gives the human persons he calls by name a share in his
messianic consecration, mission, and authority. What Jesus calls
them to is not a position of power and prestige for the ordering
of a society but rather a service for the sake of salvation. The
role of the disciples is to be different and in strict contrast to the
potentates of this world, who abuse their power over people.

The spirituality is shaped by Jesus. The apostle's admonition
is addressed to all Christians, but first and foremost to priests:
"Let the same mind be in you that was in Christ Jesus" (Phil 2:5).
Something quite different is meant by priestly spirituality than a
habit of pious sentiments and lofty gestures. Rather, the priest is
filled with the power of the Holy Spirit, with which he keeps the
good of faith and the teaching of salvation entrusted to him in
his heart, preserving it for the whole Church. The apostles and
their successors in clerical office participate in the authority of
the Lord's Anointed, Christ, the Son of God (Mk 1:1). Thus,
analogously to Jesus the Christ, it applies to each of his emissar-
ies in priestly ministry that "The Spirit of the Lord is upon me,
because he has anointed me to bring good news to the poor" (Lk
4:18; Is 61:1f.).The Spirit that priests receive in sacred ordination

is the Spirit of the Messiah (Jn 20:22), with whose authority and sending by the Father they exercise the ministry entrusted to them to sanctify, teach, and lead the Church of God. And it is through the same Spirit promised by Jesus to the whole Church at her founding (Acts 1:8, 2:4) that he gave "instructions through the Holy Spirit to the apostles whom he had chosen" (Acts 1:2) both before and after his Resurrection. Hence, all theories are *a limine* false that have attempted to construct an opposition between a Christological and a pneumatological foundation of the offices and of the Church as a whole.

The authority (*exousia*) to bring the kingdom of God in its salvific power to the people in the name of Jesus is exercised in the humility and shape of a servant or slave that was taken on by the Son of God, who emptied himself, assumed human form, and was obedient to the point of death on the Cross (cf. Phil 2:6–11).

After foretelling his Passion for the third time, when the disciples have been wasting their time squabbling about rank and are no longer unanimous, Jesus teaches them a lesson: "It will not be so among you; but whoever wishes to be great among you must be your servant, and whoever wishes to be first among you must be your slave; just as the Son of Man came not to be served but to serve, and to give his life as a ransom for many" (Mt 20:26–28). The good shepherd Jesus is the *typos* and model of the shepherds of the Church in the office of bishops and priests. Anyone exercising this pastoral office is constantly looking into the eyes of Jesus and hearing his voice appealing to his conscience. One would like to echo the words of the disciples on the road to Emmaus and ask: "Were not our hearts burning within us?" (Lk 24:32) when he called us to feed and tend his sheep and lambs (cf. Jn 21:15ff.). The one who sends us is the Son of God, who reveals the mystery of his mission and therefore of ours, too, in the words: "I am the good shepherd. The good shepherd lays down his life for the sheep. The hired hand, who is not the shepherd and does not own the sheep, sees the wolf coming and leaves the sheep and runs away" (Jn 10:11f.).

In the drama of the mission that led Jesus to his Passion and death, the salvific events of Cross and Resurrection imprint the ministry of the apostles on the Church forever in a way that is both surpassing and perfecting. Thus the whole mystery of Christ is made present through word and sign in the apostles' kerygma (cf. 1 Cor 15:1–11).

The basic elements recognizable pre-Easter of the relationship between Jesus, who is sent by the Father, and the disciples, who are sent into the world by Jesus post-Easter, too, in the service of salvation, remain completely preserved.

Jesus climbed up a mountain, thus displaying his divine authority. The apostolate consists in being called and chosen, in the freely given readiness for the *Adsum* (they came to him); in the institution into the office of each one of those called by name (which is why the names of the twelve apostles are listed individually); and in the concomitant proximity and community with the one from whom the mission and authority originate (cf. Mk 3:14, "he also named apostles, to be with him"). The aim of appointing the apostles is to send them out, to enable them to participate in his mission from the Father and in his divine authority, so that in their words Christ himself is speaking and in what they do it is Christ who is bringing about salvation. The apostles exercise their mission and authority in preaching the kingdom of God and in the powerful casting out of demons, the powers that are enemies of God and corrupt mankind both morally and physically. Corresponding to this post-Easter are the forgiveness of sins in Baptism and the work of salvation in the sacraments.

As they carry out their mission, it is said of the Twelve: "So they went out and proclaimed that all should repent. They cast out many demons, and anointed with oil many who were sick and cured them" (Mk 6:12f.).

The words of commissioning in the gospels with which the resurrected Lord sends out the apostles into the whole world merely renew their calling, mission, and empowerment in the Holy Spirit. The sending out of seventy-two further disciples

(Lk 10:1–20) in addition to the circle of the Twelve (Lk 6:12–16, 9:1–6) already points to the time after Easter when all nations enter into the radius of the Church's salvific mission. But this also already indicates that the apostolic ministry cannot be limited to the twelve disciples and end with their deaths. One must, of course, distinguish between, on the one hand, the unique importance of the disciples in testifying to the identity of the pre-paschal Jesus and crucified Messiah with the risen Lord and, on the other hand, their mission to proclaim the gospel and to work God's salvation in the sacred signs of salvation instituted by Christ.

7.

THE DEVELOPMENT OF THE SACRAMENTAL PRIESTHOOD IN THE EARLY CHURCH

THE PRIMITIVE CHURCH IN JERUSALEM

Transition from the pre-Easter community of disciples to the post-Easter Church was not accompanied by a transition from a personal mission to the material structures of a parish constitution. The personal relationship between the sender and the sent remains the essence of apostolic authority, an authority that is now passed on sacramentally. But this authority with its *munera* (that is, tasks/offices) of teaching, governing, and sanctifying is exercised within a structure composed of the various offices and their holders, which is itself sacramentally grounded.

The apostles appointed "seven men of good standing, full of the Spirit and of wisdom" to "wait at tables" and "prayed and laid their hands on them" as an effective sign (cf. Acts 6:1–6).

From Antioch, on their first missionary journey, Paul and Barnabas with apostolic authority "appointed elders [presbyters] for them in each church, [and] with prayer and fasting they entrusted them to the Lord in whom they had come to believe" (Acts 14:23). These are the elders (presbyters) who in Jerusalem together with the apostles—as their associates—reached the magisterially binding decision that those who turn to Christ do not first have to be circumcised like the Jews and adhere to the Law of Moses (cf. Acts 15:5–29).

In Paul's farewell address to the "elders" of the church of Ephesus, whom he had called together once more in Miletus, it becomes clear at the transition to the post-apostolic period that the presbyters/*episkopoi* have taken over the ministry of proclamation and leadership of the churches from the apostles. Paul transfers to them "the ministry that I received from the Lord Jesus, to testify to the good news of God's grace" (Acts 20:24). Even though they now discharge their duties in the apostolic succession, they are nevertheless still appointed to their ministry by God himself.

> Keep watch over yourselves and over all the flock, of which the Holy Spirit has made you overseers, to shepherd the church of God that he obtained with the blood of his own Son.
>
> —Acts 20:28

It is highly significant that the ministry of the presbyters or *episkopoi*, as they still stand undifferentiated alongside one another, is referred to with the biblical image of "shepherding" God's "flock." The presbyters/bishops are the elders (*prestotes presbyteroi*) "who labour in preaching and teaching" (1 Tim 5:17; cf. Heb 13:7). Like the apostles, they are shepherds who, in the authority of Christ, "the shepherd and guardian of your souls" (1 Pt 2:25), "tend the flock of God that is in your charge" (1 Pt 5:2).

Added as a new element post-Easter is their being appointed as witnesses of the salvific events of death and Resurrection: "But you will receive power when the Holy Spirit has come upon you; and you will be my witnesses in Jerusalem, in all Judea and Samaria, and to the ends of the earth" (Acts 1:8).

Their preaching no longer contains just the gospel of the kingdom of God but now also testimony to Christ's death and

Resurrection, his Ascension, the sending of the Spirit, and the Lord's return at the end of the world. What the preaching of the apostles and their successors now contains is essentially a profession of Jesus the Christ, the Messiah of the Jews and Savior of the whole of mankind. Whoever comes to faith as a result of this profession and is baptized in the name of Jesus, the Son of God and the Anointed of the Holy Spirit, will be saved. "This Jesus is 'the stone that was rejected by you, the builders; it has become the cornerstone.' There is salvation in no one else, for there is no other name under heaven given among mortals by which we must be saved" (Acts 4:11f.).

As a result of the apostles' preaching and through the working of the Spirit of Pentecost, the first community of the Lord comes into being in Jerusalem. With the apostles' mission to the Gentiles, the Church spreads over the whole world. It is the visible community of faith that we profess as the one, holy, catholic, and apostolic Church.

ORIGIN AND MEANING OF ST. PAUL'S APOSTOLATE

In the letters he addresses to the churches he has founded, Paul gives us an insight into the life of the early Christians. His communities were the result of his missionary journeys. In the spread of the Church among the diaspora Jews and the Gentiles (Hellenes, Greeks) the universality/catholicity of the Church became a reality both intensively and extensively. God's universal salvific will is revealed in the Church's spreading out through all the world.

Apostolicity and catholicity are crucial characteristics of God's one, holy Church, "a people made one with the unity of the Father, the Son and the Holy Spirit" (LG 4).

The question of the historical development of the structures of the Pauline communities is a superficial one. For Paul, the Church is not what we can capture with sociological criteria.

The Church is the one Body of Christ with its many members. Her physical shape in the assembly of the saints is the making present of the sacred and sanctifying presence of God, Jesus Christ, and the Holy Spirit. "Now there are varieties of gifts, but the same Spirit; and there are varieties of services, but the same Lord; and there are varieties of activities, but it is the same God who activates all of them in everyone" (1 Cor 12:4ff.).

That is why it is wrong to go along with the dualistic scheme of "charism and institution" propounded in liberal Protestant theology in assuming that Paul's communities had a charismatic constitution based solely on a supernatural working of the Spirit and that this was later replaced by institutions and offices in the sociological-political sense (Rudolf Sohm) as the working of the Spirit diminished. The sociological categories of charismatic, traditional, and rational legitimation of authority such as we find in the sociologist Max Weber do not lead us anywhere here. What is called charismatic-secularist here has nothing to do with the charismatic-supernatural gifts of the Holy Spirit.[13]

For the authority is God, who works through the apostle in and for the Church in combination with the charisms and ministries of all the baptized, who with their natural talents and free gifts of the Spirit help to support the life and the mission of the Church. From the very beginning until today the Church has had a sacramental-charismatic constitution. In Baptism, the charisms of the "laity," too, are sacramentally grounded; likewise the work of the apostles and their successors in the office of bishops and priests in both Baptism and the Sacrament of Holy Orders. "For in the one Spirit we were all baptized into one body [. . .] and we were all made to drink of one Spirit. Indeed, the body does not consist of one member but of many" (1 Cor 12:13f.).

For the paramount importance of the apostles for laying the foundations of the Church and her lasting constitution does not stand in any kind of opposition to the gifts of the Spirit granted to individual Christians that shape the whole life and work of the Church when used in union with one another. The apostle did not found local churches and then leave them to fend for themselves. That would have been a kind of ecclesiological Deism, which, although it acknowledged God as the Creator of the world, would teach that he then left the world to run like clockwork and now allowed the ecclesial organization to take its own course.

When founding their churches, the apostles at the same time planted in them an apostolic principle that continually builds up the life and shape of the apostolic Church through fidelity to the teachings of the apostles and the mission and authority of their successors. It is a question of the sacramentality of the Church or whether the Church is simply a community of ideas which, regardless of its essence as the presence of God in the Body of Christ, can give itself varying forms of external organization that will always remain extrinsic to this essence. No, what we have is not a disorganized sum of all the baptized giving itself—as it were from secular considerations—some form of external organization. If the Church is the Body of Christ, then the persons who serve in building her up are also invested with their authority and competence by God.

Unity and plurality in the Church do not relate to one another like a basic idea and the various shapes it takes. Rather, it is the one and the same Christ who joins the many Christians to himself and to one another in the same way as the head joins the many members into the unity of one body. It is about the presence of Christ in the many persons who make up the one Church and the Church as one single person, that is, the bride of Christ and the mother of all the faithful. The multiplicity of Christians in the one Church are joined together into a unity by the God who is One in Three Persons. And among the various ministries instituted by God and the variety of charisms with which people are endowed over and over again, there is also the office of apostle, which exercises the office of unity in the name of God and maintains the Church in the truth of the gospel. Part of it is also the examination, recognition, and fostering of spiritual gifts (1 Cor 14:12–26, 38ff.).

That makes those who are "servants of Christ and stewards of God's mysteries" (1 Cor 4:1) and "God's servants, working together; [. . .] God's field, God's building" (1 Cor 3:9) independent of human judgment. "Moreover, it is required of stewards that they should be found trustworthy. But with me it is a very small thing that I should be judged by you or by any human court. I do not even judge myself. I am not aware of anything against myself, but I am not thereby acquitted" (1 Cor 4:2ff.).

So let every priest say like the apostle in the certainty of his mission and in his honest examination of conscience: "It is the Lord who judges me" (1 Cor 4:4).

"For just as the body is one and has many members, and all the members of the body, though many, are one body, so it is with Christ" (1 Cor 12:12). "And God has appointed in the church first apostles, second prophets, third teachers; then deeds of power, then gifts of healing, forms of assistance, forms of leadership, various kinds of tongues. Are all apostles? Are all prophets? Are all teachers? Do all work miracles? Do all possess gifts of healing? Do all speak in tongues? Do all interpret? But strive for the greater gifts" (1 Cor 12:28–31a; cf. Rom 12:3–8).

Principles of Unity

Working together in a well-ordered manner, the hierarchical offices and the charismatic gifts (cf. *LG* 12) serve to build up the Body of Christ. That is a fundamental ecclesiological principle. Different tasks demand different offices and persons. However, their working together in the Holy Spirit also calls for a corresponding office of unity: in the local church it is the bishop and in the universal Church it is the pope. Paul emphasizes that his apostolate comes directly from the resurrected Christ, saying he is "an apostle—sent neither by human commission nor from human authorities, but through Jesus Christ and God the Father, who raised him from the dead" (Gal 1:1). Consequently Paul also received the gospel directly from Jesus (cf. Gal 1:12). This puts him on the same level as the apostles, the twelve disciples who were called personally by the earthly Jesus and whose apostolate was confirmed by the risen Lord and had been expanded into a universal mission (1 Cor 15:1–5). This is also what distinguishes their apostolate from that of the successors of the apostles in the offices of bishop and priest: it is only through the mediation of the apostles in the sacrament consisting of consecratory prayer and the imposition of hands that they are empowered to act in the person of Christ through the power of the Holy Spirit in the service of salvation.

So the apostles are to be regarded "as servants of Christ and stewards of God's mysteries" (1 Cor 4:1). They "work together with him" (2 Cor 6:1) and "are God's servants, working together" while "you are God's field, God's building" (1 Cor 3:9). All the apostles collaborate in different phases of building up God's one Church, knowing that it is "only God who gives the growth [. . .] and each will receive wages according to the labour of each" (1 Cor 3:7f.). That is an exact description of how the sacraments work. The priest performs the visible sacred symbolic actions, and God invisibly effects the grace they symbolize through his servant (cf. 2 Cor 5:20).

The relationship between apostle and community is one of origin and cannot be reversed. This basic principle of the apostolic also has an impact on the shaping of the ministry of bishops and presbyters. The letters authorized in Paul's name present his coworkers Timothy and Titus as prototypes of ecclesial officeholders. Here we are at the transition to the post-apostolic period that follows the laying of the Church's foundations by "the apostles and prophets" (Eph 2:20; cf. Eph 3:5; Rev 21:14). The Church is "built upon the foundation of the apostles and prophets, with Christ Jesus himself as the cornerstone. In him the whole structure is joined together and grows into a holy temple in the Lord; in whom you also are built together spiritually into a dwelling-place for God" (Eph 2:20–22).

After the apostles in the primitive Church, it is from then on the "pastors and teachers" who are appointed by Christ in the Holy Spirit "for building up the body of Christ" (Eph 4:11).

They are the presbyters (elders) "who labour in preaching and teaching" (1 Tim 5:17). The successor of the apostles is the bishop, who takes care of the household of God's church (cf. 1 Tim 3:5). This house built by God (cf. Heb 3:3f.) is identical with "the church of the living God, the pillar and bulwark of the truth" (1 Tim 3:15), regarding which he adds: "Without any doubt, the mystery of our religion is great" (1 Tim 3:16). About the apostles Paul says: "Think of us in this way, as servants of Christ and stewards (*oikonomoi*) of God's mysteries" (1 Cor 4:1). Likewise the bishop (overseer) is now "God's steward (*oikonom tou Theou*)" (Ti 1:7). For this reason "He must have a firm grasp of the word that is trustworthy in accordance with the teaching, so that he may be able both to preach with sound doctrine and to refute those who contradict it" (Ti 1:9).

So the apostolic teaching is only entrusted to the episcopal teacher in order for him to preserve it faithfully, not to arbitrarily reinterpret it according to paradigms he has invented himself in a time that is coming "when people will not put up with sound doctrine, but having itching ears, they will accumulate for themselves teachers to suit their own desires" (2 Tim 4:3).

WHAT IS THE PRINCIPLE OF APOSTOLICITY AND THE APOSTOLIC SUCCESSION IN THE OFFICE OF BISHOP?

The faith that brings us salvation is founded on the word of Christ, "(that is, the word of faith that we proclaim); because if you confess with your lips that Jesus is Lord and believe in your heart that God raised him from the dead, you will be saved. [. . .] For, 'Everyone who calls on the name of the Lord shall be saved'" (Rom 10:8b–13). "So faith comes from what is heard, and what is heard comes through the word of Christ" (Rom 10:17) passed on through the message of the apostles. Of the apostles Paul says: "So we are ambassadors for Christ, since God is making his appeal through us" (2 Cor 5:20). Thus there exists a sequence of causes effecting the justification of the sinner and his adoption by God as a son. But this last effect of ecclesial mission originates from the same God who is the one who has called, chosen, and commissioned the ambassadors of the gospel.

So Paul defines the apostolate as serving the mediation of salvation:

> But how are they to call on one in whom they have not believed? And how are they to believe in one of whom they have never heard? And how are they to hear without someone to proclaim him? And how are they to proclaim him unless they are sent? As it is written, "How beautiful are the feet of those who bring good news!"
>
> —Romans 10:14f.

The apostles are sent into the world to proclaim the gospel of Christ so that those who hear them come, through faith, to worship and glorify God.

That is the apostolate as the element that defines the essence of the Church's constitution.

It is the passing on of the sending of Christ by the Father to the apostles (Jn 20:21ff.) and the sending of the apostles to the bishops (Acts 6:3, 14:23, 20:28; 1 Tim 1:16, 3:10; 2 Tim 2:1; Ti 1:5). The sending out of the apostles had its roots in the sending of the Son of God, "and both these things were done in good order, according to the will of God" (*1 Clem* 42,2). Part of the proclamation of the gospel through which they founded the churches was to entrust "what you have heard from me [. . .] to faithful people who will be able to teach others as well" (2 Tim 2:2; cf. *1 Clem* 44,3). So "they appointed their first fruits to be bishops and deacons over such as should believe, after they had proved them in the Spirit" (*1 Clem* 42,4).

This in substance expresses clearly and unambiguously the principle of apostolic succession and the teaching authority of the bishops as heads of the individual churches. This principle is then soon developed by Irenaeus of Lyon into a comprehensive theological approach to counter the muddled speculations of the Gnostics. "Wherefore it is incumbent to obey the presbyters who are in the Church—those who, as I have shown, possess the succession from the apostles; those who, together with the succession of the episcopate (*episcopatu successione*), have received the certain gift of truth, according to the good pleasure of the Father" (*Epideixis* 3). And he continues: "But [it is also incumbent] to hold in suspicion others who depart from the primitive succession, and assemble themselves together in any place whatsoever, [looking upon them] either as heretics of perverse minds, or as schismatics" (*Haer.* 4,26,1). The "origin" of the episcopal succession has a horizontal point of departure in the apostles, but also a vertical one in that Christ as the founder of the historical apostolate of the bishops as successors to the apostles allows them through their consecration in the Holy Spirit to share in his own mission and authority (cf. Mt 28:18ff.).

The doctrine of the apostolic succession of the episcopate cannot be explained as an ahistorical fiction that was only constructed for the controversy with Gnosticism. Nor does it by any means cut the ground from under the doctrine if no documentary evidence can be provided that traces the calling of every single bishop back to a specific apostle. It is enough to have the witness of the biblical scriptures and the documents immediately following them which testify to the Church's belief that the authority of the bishops not only goes back historically to the time of the apostolic foundations of the Church but is also "transcendentally" anchored in Christ's working in the present time. The Exalted Lord is always with his Church until the end of the age. He himself causes the apostolic authority and mission to continue even after the death of the twelve apostles, the seventy-two disciples, the apostle Paul and his coworkers

Timothy, Titus, Silvanus, and Sosthenes (1 Cor 1:1), and the other primitive Christian missionaries, evangelists, and prophets.

But even when the historical events are looked at in a purely linear fashion, there is abundant historical evidence of the provenance of the bishops from the apostles.

Paul praises the glorious nature of his service of the new covenant, but he does not boast about himself. "Knowing the fear of the Lord," all he wants to do is to "try to persuade others" (2 Cor 5:11) for Christ. The ministry assigned to him by God's mercy arouses an unflagging zeal for proclamation and pastoral care (2 Cor 4:1).

Only in this way can the apostle survive the hardships and hopes of his apostolic office. Like him, we, too, get the impression "that God has exhibited us apostles as last of all [. . .] because we have become a spectacle to the world, to angels and to mortals" (1 Cor 4:9).

And at the heart of priestly spirituality is this: "For we do not proclaim ourselves; we proclaim Jesus Christ as Lord and ourselves as your slaves for Jesus' sake. For it is the God who said, 'Let light shine out of darkness,' who has shone in our hearts to give the light of the knowledge of the glory of God in the face of Jesus Christ. But we have this treasure in clay jars, so that it may be made clear that this extraordinary power belongs to God and does not come from us. [. . .] Yes, everything is for your sake, so that grace, as it extends to more and more people, may increase thanksgiving, to the glory of God" (2 Cor 4:5–15).

This attitude prevents the priest from becoming a functionary or even worse a hired hand who "does not care for the sheep" (Jn 10:13). Anyone who offers Christ's sacrifice daily in his person together with and for the faithful will sacrifice himself in his ministry according to the example of the Son of Man, who "came not to be served but to serve, and to give his life as a ransom for many" (Mk 10:45).

The ontological *character indelebilis* of the ordained priesthood, that is, the indelible character grounded in the reality of grace, is disputed in controversial theology and not understood by modernist Catholics. In fact it is nothing more than the inner configuration of the priest to Christ, the good shepherd, who risked his life for his sheep, just as each of the baptized is in reality and not fictitiously conformed to Christ, who "came as a high priest of the good things that have come, [. . .] thus obtaining eternal redemption" (Heb 9:11f.).

Christ himself imprints the indelible seal on the one who represents him as head of the Church. It would be Pelagianism to say that the imprinting of the sacramental seal in Baptism, Confirmation, and Holy Orders depended on the subjective holiness and moral and spiritual performance of the recipient of these sacraments.

8.

THE ECCLESIAL SHAPING OF THE PRIESTLY OFFICE IN THE POST-APOSTOLIC PERIOD

Dear Confreres and Fellow Christians,

If the Church of Christ interprets the word of God in sacred scripture in the same spirit in which she heard, interpreted, and recorded it in writing, then the Old and New Testaments are for her an eternally flowing wellspring, guideline, and source of nourishment on her pilgrimage towards a complete knowledge and love of God.

The New Testament displays an inner unity and reflects the homogeneous development of the ordained priesthood from its primitive apostolic shape to the Church's dogmatic formulation of its essence in the phase following her apostolic foundation.

The gospels and the Acts of the Apostles provide evidence of the institution of the apostolate. In all the nuances of the development of the term "apostle" and its application to the Twelve, to Paul and his apostolic collaborators, and to the seventy-two and others belonging to this circle, the apostle is always a person who through the authority of the Holy Spirit shares in Jesus' sending by the Father and continues it into the foundation of the Church, which is one as a visible community in her teaching, life, and constitution.

119

In the mission of the apostle Paul as he himself portrays it in his letters and as it is testified to in Luke's Acts of the Apostles, we see the fundamental importance of the apostolate for the formation and evolution of the local churches. The apostolic coworkers mentioned in the letters such as Sosthenes, Apollos, Barnabas, Titus, Epaphroditus (Phil 2:25), and Timothy, who "is doing the work of the Lord just as I am" (1 Cor 16:10), and the first overseers in the local communities all point us to Paul's successors in apostolic ministry, who as God's coworkers and servants of Christ proclaim the gospel and are stewards of the mysteries of divine grace.

"Paul, Silvanus, and Timothy" (1 Thess 1:1) appeal to the Christians of the community in Thessalonica "to respect those who labour among you, and have charge of you in the Lord and admonish you; esteem them very highly in love because of their work" (1 Thess 5:12f.; cf. Rom 12:8). They, like their helpers and coworkers, are urged to "put yourselves at the service of such people, and of everyone who works and toils with them. [. . .] So give recognition to such people" (1 Cor 16:16–18; cf. Gal 6:6; Col 4:17; Heb 13:17; *1 Clem* 57,1; *IgnMag* 13,2).

Paul and Timothy address the Letter to the Philippians (ca. AD 55) "To all the saints in Christ Jesus who are in Philippi, with the bishops and deacons" (Phil 1:1). This is the first mention of the terms that were to develop into precise designations for specific offices in the course of Acts and the pastoral epistles. In introductions to biblical studies and exegesis people speak quite rightly of a development in the terminology as well as the more precise content of the early Christian office of overseer. This genesis of the understanding of the office must not, however, be allowed to lead to false conclusions based on the dogmatic and historical premises of Protestant dogmatics and liberal historiography. *Episkopos, presbyteros,* and *diakonos* are not secular designations that were later charged with sacred meaning that was in contrast to their original Christian meaning. In the Septuagint, in the New Testament (1 Pt 2:25), and in the early Christian literature (*IgnMag* 3,1), even God and Christ are occasionally referred to as bishop (*episkopos*). The term *episkopos* is actually a synonym for the metaphor of the shepherd, which is God and Christ, and is applied to those who feed God's flock in Christ's name as good shepherds (*1 Clem* 54,2). The elders/presbyters and Levites received the spirit and the power of God in order to lead the people (cf. Num 8:10, 11:16f., 11:24, 27:18–23; Deut 34:9) through the laying on of hands and the prayers of Moses and Aaron. The seventy elders (presbyters) from among the people on whom the Lord put some of the spirit that was on Moses (cf. Num 11:25) are reminiscent of the seventy(-two) additional disciples whom Jesus, the Lord of the harvest, had called so as to send them out as laborers in his harvest (cf. Lk 10:1–16). And the word "deacon" expresses the innermost essence of Christ's saving mission. Hence all offices in the Church are in their very being and essence "diakonia" (*LG* 24).

The different degrees of participation in the one apostolic ministry and thus the specific characteristics of bishop, presbyter, and deacon are not the result of some arbitrary decree or purely factual tradition; rather, they come about along with the formation of the local churches and the one apostolic office directed towards their needs. The unity of origin of this office is represented in the bishop and the plurality of its bearers is realized in the presbyters and deacons.

In the Letter of James "To the twelve tribes in the Dispersion" (Jas 1:1), the ministry of the "priests of the Church" who mediate real salvation "in the name of Christ" appears as an institution that is taken for granted. Their ministry to the sick, which is what is being discussed here, has a sacramental dimension. A visible sign effects an invisible healing. "Are any among you sick? They should call for the elders [presbyters] of the church and have them pray over them, anointing them with oil in the name of the Lord. The prayer of faith will save the sick, and the Lord will raise them up; and anyone who has committed sins will be forgiven" (Jas 5:14f.).

Acts, the three pastoral epistles, and the First Letter of Peter give evidence of the advanced development of the ministries of the *episkopoi*/presbyters and deacons, which, founded as they were in the tradition of the primitive Church, were already taking on their own distinctive shape between AD 70 and AD 90. These constitute the immediate precursors of the three-part office that the Church in her reflective faith awareness sees as the result of her being accompanied by the Holy Spirit (*divina ordinatione*). Comparable with this is the recognition of the early Christian writings as the word of God and that they belong to the canon.

In a local church that is part of the universal Church, the apostolic office's unity in its apostolic origin is represented by a bishop while its community nature is represented by the plurality of presbyters in the one presbyterium. This unity in plurality guarantees the organic whole of the one body of the Church under Christ, her head. In a systematic reflection, Thomas Aquinas distinguishes the still-fluid terminology from the objective distinction between a bishop as *summus sacerdos* and the presbyter as *sacerdos simplex* that is inherent in the nature of the unified office. "But as regards the thing signified by these terms, there was always a difference between them, even at the time of the apostles." Following the medieval exegetical tradition, Thomas points to the difference between the calling of the twelve apostles and the other seventy-two disciples. "But to assert that priests nowise differ from bishops is reckoned by Augustine among heretical doctrines (cf. *Haer.* 53), where he says that the Arians maintained that 'no distinction existed between a priest and a bishop'" (*S.th.* II-II q.184 a.6 ad 1).

We first come across this Christologically and ecclesiologically reasoned constitution of the Church in the letters of St. Ignatius of Antioch at the beginning of the second century. In Paul's pastoral epistles, Timothy and Titus appear as the prototypes of the bishops of a local church. They have the function of overseeing the bishops/presbyters they have ordained. However, in this phase of transition to the post-apostolic Church they possess even more the apostle's responsibility for the universal Church, which means that in their own person they link the apostolic with the post-apostolic phase of Church history. Timothy and Titus, erstwhile preeminent coworkers of Paul who "was appointed as a herald and an apostle [. . .], a teacher of the Gentiles in faith and truth" (1 Tim 2:7), are entrusted with guarding the "apostles' teaching" (Acts 2:42), that is, the "sound teaching" that is summarized in the Creed, the *depositum fidei* (cf. 1 Tim 4:16, 6:20; 2 Tim 1:14). Nevertheless it is precisely the example of Timothy and Titus that demonstrates how a bishop bound to the local church bore responsibility for the magisterium and community of the universal Church as well. The apostle Paul's exhortation to Timothy applies to every bishop as a successor of the apostles: "Do your best to present yourself to God as one approved by him, a worker who has no need to be ashamed, rightly explaining the word of truth. [. . .] And the Lord's servant must not be quarrelsome but kindly to everyone, an apt teacher, patient, correcting opponents with gentleness" (2 Tim 2:15, 2:24).

The bishop/presbyter who is to be a steward of the House of God must be free from vices and possess the natural virtues of an upright man (cf. 1 Tim 3:2; Ti 1:5–9). Therefore "He must have a firm grasp of the word that is trustworthy in accordance with the teaching, so that he may be able both to preach with sound doctrine and to refute those who contradict it" (Ti 1:9).

THE SHAPING OF THE PRIESTLY OFFICE IN THE SECOND CENTURY

The "Epistle of the Church at Rome to the Church at Corinth" (*1 Clem* 1,1) represents a kind of transition between the last biblical writings and the letters of Ignatius. Even though the differentiation between the office of bishop and the presbyters subordinate to him has not yet been completely clarified here, the epistle does already enunciate the principle of apostolic succession that Irenaeus of Lyon was later, after his stay in Rome (ca. AD 177), to incorporate and give a final shape to in his comprehensive hermeneutics of the Catholic faith. Irenaeus combines the Eastern with the Western tradition in the same way as the *Traditio Apostolica* of Hippolytus (ca. AD 220) expresses the unity of faith in the Roman and Alexandrine ordination liturgies.

It is certain that since the time of the apostles the gift of the Holy Spirit has been conferred on bishops and presbyters through the laying on of hands and prayer (cf. 2 Tim 1:6–14) so that through their word the word of Christ is spoken and awakens the faith of the hearers, and that in the sacraments they both symbolically and efficaciously pass on Christ's grace.

The ministry of the bishop and presbyter belongs to the apostolic constitution. It was instituted by the apostles (cf. *1 Clem* 42,4; 44,1), and whoever contests the authority given them by God destroys the divine order (cf. *1 Clem* 46,6; 47,5). Anyone who aspires to this office in order to serve the Church and not himself "desires a noble task" (1 Tim 3:1).

The two testaments of the apostles Peter and Paul to the overseers of the churches they had founded in the First Letter of Peter and in Acts offer a parallel in their ecclesiology and official theology as far as the history of the tradition is concerned. They reflect more or less the same stage of development, namely that between AD 70 and AD 90. In the First Letter of Peter, which is likely to have been written in Rome, so that the Roman Petrine tradition is discernible in it, the apostle, as a fellow presbyter, ranks the presbyters alongside himself. The overseers of the churches work in the name of Christ, "the shepherd and guardian of your souls" (1 Pt 2:25). Jesus is the "chief shepherd" (1 Pt 5:4; cf. Heb 13:20; Jn 10:11 with Jn 21:15). The essence of the mission of bishops and presbyters is most clearly described as a pastoral office embracing all the tasks of teaching, governing, and sanctifying: "to tend the flock of God that is in your charge, exercising the oversight, not under compulsion but willingly, as God would have you do it—not for sordid gain but eagerly. Do not lord it over those in your charge, but be examples to the flock—*forma facti gregis ex animo*" (1 Pt 5:2f.; *1 Clem* 16,1).

In his farewell words to the elders of the church of Ephesus, Paul entrusts his apostolic teaching to the presbyters whom he had appointed "with prayer and fasting" (Acts 14:23). And he expects of them that after his death they will carry out the ministry that was assigned to the apostle himself by the Lord Jesus, namely "to testify to the good news of God's grace" (Acts 20:24). And now he describes the nature and mission of the bishops/presbyters in the way we have just heard it from Peter: "Keep watch over yourselves and over all the flock, of which the Holy Spirit has made you overseers [bishops], to shepherd the church of God that he obtained with the blood of his own Son" (Acts 20:28).

The image of the three-part office that we encounter in the writings of St. Ignatius of Antioch does not represent a new concept but rather the conclusion of a development: "[B]ishops, settled everywhere to the utmost bounds [of the earth], are so by the will of Jesus Christ" (*IgnEph* 3,2). Of inner necessity, the seed brings forth the fruit that already genetically preexisted in it before appearing as a phenotype. The unity is typologically grounded in the fact that the bishop stands in the place of God whereas the presbyters represent the plurality of the apostles when they preside at the Church assembly, and the "deacons, who are most dear to me, [. . .] are entrusted with the ministry of Jesus Christ" (*IgnMag* 6,1) there. The sacramental nature of the episcopal office is clearly expressed in the fact that the visible bishop represents God and Christ as the invisible bishop and true shepherd of the Church, preaching, baptizing, and presiding in the Church and at the Eucharist in his name for our salvation (cf. *IgnMag* 3,1f.; 6,2; 13,1f.; *IgnTrall* 2,2; 3,1).

Ignatius is far from trying to promote a community model that he himself had invented. Even though in his letter to the Romans he does not address their local bishop, and the office of the chief pastor among the many pastors may not yet have been defined with the clarity otherwise customary in Ignatius, he does speak in the letter of the episcopal office in his understanding of it (*IgnRom* 2,2; 9,1).

It would be a complete misunderstanding of what Ignatius is intending to say to speak of a transition from collegial leadership of the community to a monarchical episcopate. There has always been the one single origin of all offices, namely in being sent by Christ. And this was represented by the apostle or by his pupils such as Timothy and Titus. But it in no way contradicts the plurality and collegiality of the overseers of a local church that one of them, who is now called exclusively a bishop, represents their unity and, as a successor to the apostles, guarantees the legitimacy of their authority and mission in that he performs the sacred ordinations.

Ignatius is thus less concerned with possessing a higher or lower rank than with the unity and community of all the faithful and pastors with their episcopal chief pastor in a spirit of love: "For your justly renowned presbytery, worthy of God, is fitted as exactly to the bishop as the strings are to the harp" (*IgnEph* 4,1). The Roman church had already written to the church in Corinth: "only let the flock of Christ be at peace together with the appointed presbyters" (*1 Clem* 54,2), for: "Have we not one God and one Christ? Is not the Spirit of grace, which was poured out upon us, one? Is not our calling one in Christ? Why do we tear apart and rend asunder the members of Christ, and make sedition against our body, and come to such a degree of madness that we forget we are members one of another?" (*1 Clem* 46,6f.). And Ignatius has the same concern: "Do nothing without the bishop; [. . .] love unity; avoid divisions" (*IgnPhil* 7,2).

In order to show that the Church's constitution is not sociologically and politically founded, but rather ecclesially and eucharistically, it suffices to quote just one passage that sheds complete light on the sacramental office as a constitutive element of the Catholic Church.

> See that you all follow the bishop, even as Jesus Christ does the Father, and the presbytery as you would the apostles; and reverence the deacons, as being the institution of God. Let no man do anything connected with the Church without the bishop. Let that

be deemed a proper Eucharist, which is [adminis-
tered] either by the bishop, or by one to whom he
has entrusted it. Wherever the bishop shall appear,
there let the multitude [of the people] also be; even
as, wherever Jesus Christ is, there is the Catholic
Church. It is not lawful without the bishop either to
baptize or to celebrate a love-feast; but whatsoever
he shall approve of, that is also pleasing to God, so
that everything that is done may be secure and valid.
(*IgnSmy* 8,1–2)

The unity of the Church is grounded in the Eucharist, which
is why it is in the person of the bishop that the service of unity
finds its expression. The fact that only the bishop and presbyters
can preside at the Eucharist and validly offer up the eucharistic sacrifice is not the result of some canonical disciplinary
regulation but is grounded in the nature of priesthood and the
inner relationship between the ecclesial and sacramental Body
of Christ.

"Take heed, then, to have but one Eucharist. For there is
one flesh of our Lord Jesus Christ, and one cup to [show forth]
the unity of His blood; one altar; as there is one bishop, along
with the presbytery and deacons, my fellow-servants: that so,
whatsoever you do, you may do it according to [the will of] God"
(*IgnPhil* 4). And "He that is within the altar is pure, but he that
is without is not pure; that is, he who does anything apart from
the bishop, and presbytery, and deacons, such a man is not pure
in his conscience" (*IgnTrall* 7,2).

Against the heresy of the Cathars and Albigensians the
Fourth Lateran Council (1215) used the same line of thought
to justify the restriction of the authority to consecrate the Eucharist to the ordained priest alone: "There is indeed one universal
Church of the faithful outside of which no one at all is saved
and in which the priest himself, Jesus Christ, is also the sacrifice.
His Body and Blood are truly contained in the sacrament of the
altar under the appearances of bread and wine, the bread being
transubstantiated into the body by the divine power and the

wine into the blood. Indeed, no one can perform this sacrament except the priest duly ordained (*rite ordinatus*) according to [the power of] the keys of the Church, which Jesus Christ himself conceded to the apostles and their successors" (DH 802).

The Church does not capture her own essence, mission, and hierarchical constitution by absolutizing her external appearance at one particular stage of her development; instead she must grasp the real idea inherent in them, distinguishing between institutions of divine and of human canon law (for example, the distinction between the degrees of sacramental ordination and the non-sacramental ministries).

The real idea of the sacramental ordo of bishop, priest, and deacon is the either total or graduated participation in the mission and authority of Christ entrusted by him to the apostles (cf. *LG* 20), appointing them "to feed the Church in Christ's name with the word and the grace of God" (*LG* 11).

It is characteristic and highly significant that it was not in the form of a solemn doctrinal decision that the Church first set down what had been garnered from the biblical foundation and historical development of the Sacrament of Holy Orders but rather in the witness of the ordination liturgy. The liturgy is, according to the principle of *lex orandi—lex credendi* (DH 246), a primordial representation of the faith which often even surpasses doctrinal decisions in its value as a source. Prayed faith is richer than how it is rendered in theological reflection. We find the faith awareness regarding the sacramental ordination of bishop, presbyter, and deacon fully expressed in the *Traditio Apostolica* of Hippolytus (early third century). This not only sums up what had hitherto developed but also sets out the lasting norm for the future of the Church for all time.

The bishop is called high priest (*archiereus/primatum sacerdotii habens*) in community with the presbyters because the high priest Christ acts through him and he "offers the gifts of the Church" in the liturgy. Linguistic reference to Christ as high priest of the new covenant and to those who perform the ministry of reconciliation and offer the eucharistic sacrifice in his place is, of course, older (*Did.* 13,3; *1 Clem* 36,1; 40,5; 44,4). In the translations of the Letter to the Hebrews into Old Latin, Christ the high priest is also rendered as *pontifex*, which in this way became the title for the priest and bishop as *summus pontifex*. What is meant by this is not a moderator who reconciles various and contradictory opinions via group dynamics but rather one who mediates salvation in the name of Jesus. The pontifex here is Christ, the mediator between God and humanity, who exercises his priesthood in the Church through the sacramental ministry of the bishops and presbyters. The ancient Roman title of *pontifex maximus* is likely to have been political in origin and has nothing to do with the sacerdotal titles of bishop and presbyter, which are on the contrary of Christian origin.

THE LITURGY OF ORDERS IN THE *TRADITIO APOSTOLICA*

The still-valid teaching on sacramental orders and the consecratory ordination of bishop, priest, and deacon is comprehensively and normatively recorded in Hippolytus's *Traditio Apostolica*.

In accordance with the Old Testament model, ordination takes place with the laying on of hands by the bishop and the consecratory prayer (*TA* 2). The prayer is addressed to the Father and requests the descent of the Holy Spirit, whom the Son of the Father Jesus Christ already bestowed on the apostles (*TA* 3). Whoever is chosen by God for the office of bishop in order to feed God's flock and, as a high priest, to offer God the gifts of Holy Church, to forgive sins, and, in the authority of the apostles, to distribute the offices in the various orders receives in ordination "the spirit of high priesthood" (*TA* 3) through which his human words and symbolic acts are made effective with God.

The bishop receives his ordination from other bishops; the priest is ordained by the bishop alone. But because of the same shared spirit that binds them together in the presbyterium, the presbyters who are present should also lay their hands on the prospective presbyter being ordained. "The presbyter has only the authority to receive this spirit, but he has no authority to give it. Therefore he does not ordain any clergy. Upon the ordination of the presbyter he seals by laying on his hands, whereas the bishop alone ordains" (*TA* 8). With respect to their priestly ministry, bishop and presbyter differ only in that the overall leadership of the Church is conferred on the bishop, which is why he alone performs all ordinations so as to guarantee the supernatural unity of the Church in God and the unity of the apostolic succession.

At his ordination the presbyter receives "the spirit of grace and the wisdom of the presbytery, so that he may help and guide God's people with a pure heart" (*TA* 7). And the bishop asks the Lord "that the spirit of his grace may be unceasingly (*indeficienter*) preserved in us" (*TA* 7). The supreme realization of the priesthood of the bishop and the presbyters occurs when bishop and presbyters say the Eucharistic Prayer together in thanksgiving for all God's salvific deeds and to the glory of the Father through Jesus Christ in the Holy Spirit (*TA* 4). "Therefore, remembering his death and resurrection, we offer to you the bread and the chalice (*memores offerimus*), giving thanks to you, who has made us worthy to stand before you and to serve as your priests" (*TA* 4; cf. Justin, 1 *Apol.* 65).

The deacons are ordained by the bishop not for the priesthood but to the service of the bishop (*TA* 8). But they, too, within the framework of their tasks, represent Christ in his salvific ministry (*IgnMag* 6,1; *IgnTrall* 2,3) and differ from the laity and from other non-sacramental offices in the Church, beginning with that of the sub-deacon (*TA* 13).

The further history of dogma and theology merely clarifies individual questions, goes into greater systematic depth, and develops a speculative penetration of the real idea of the Sacrament of Holy Orders. There is no need here to go into individual questions and controversies. I am thinking, for example, of the following: whether there is a dogmatic or merely a jurisdictional difference between presbyterate and episcopate;

whether the episcopate represents a sacramental degree of ordination of its own; whether the material of the act of ordination is the handing over of the appropriate cultic equipment or merely the imposition of hands; whether from the nature of the sacrament only baptized males can validly receive the sacrament; whether heretics can validly administer and receive the sacrament; whether and in what manner it also belongs to the objective effect of the sacrament that it is unrepeatable (*character indelebilis*), an aspect explored above all by St. Augustine against the Donatists.

All these questions presuppose the basic structure as we find it in the ordination liturgies modelled on the apostolic tradition rather than questioning it.

THE COLLABORATION OF BISHOP, PRIEST, AND DEACON

Within the framework of a comprehensive presentation of its teaching on the nature and mission of the Church, the Second Vatican Council, as it were, summed up the hierarchical, that is, sacramental, constitution of the Church. Chapter 3 of *Lumen Gentium* outlines the origin of the three-part office from the sending of Christ and of the apostles. From this result the founding of the Sacrament of Holy Orders by Christ and its efficacy in the Holy Spirit. "Bishops, therefore, with their helpers, the priests and deacons, have taken up the service of the community, presiding in place of God over the flock, whose shepherds they are, as teachers for doctrine, priests for sacred worship, and ministers for governing" (*LG* 20). A detailed description of the origin, nature, and specific tasks of the sacramental episcopal office is followed in Art. 28 by a portrayal of the presbyterate and concludes with the diaconate in Art. 29.

> Priests, although they do not possess the highest degree of the priesthood, and although they are dependent on the bishops in the exercise of their

power, nevertheless they are united with the bishops in sacerdotal dignity. By the power of the sacrament of orders, in the image of Christ the eternal high priest (cf. Heb 5:1–10; 7:24; 9:11–28), they are consecrated to preach the Gospel and shepherd the faithful and to celebrate divine worship, so that they are true priests of the New Testament. Partakers of the function of Christ the sole mediator (cf. 1 Tim 2:5), on their level of ministry, they announce the divine word to all. They exercise their sacred function especially in the eucharistic worship or the celebration of the Mass by which, acting in the person of Christ and proclaiming his Mystery, they unite the prayers of the faithful with the sacrifice of their Head and renew and apply in the sacrifice of the Mass until the coming of the Lord (cf. 1 Cor 11:26) the only sacrifice of the New Testament namely that of Christ offering himself once for all a spotless Victim to the Father (cf. Heb 9:11–28). For the sick and the sinners among the faithful, they exercise the ministry of alleviation and reconciliation and they present the needs and the prayers of the faithful to God the Father. (cf. Heb 5:1–4) (*LG* 28)

Linked to this is the whole sphere of fatherly pastoral care for the community entrusted to them and for its individual members, sharing their hopes and cares like a good shepherd and kind teacher. Priests should not only set a moral example in their private lives, but should in public, too, as good and faithful pastors, be "typical," like a second Christ, as role models for their flock. To this belongs caring for lukewarm Catholics and the many people outside the Church who are seeking the truth that only God can be in order to discover the inalienable meaning of their lives. But priests should also, under the leadership of the bishops and the supreme pontiff, carry the spirit and love of Christ as a potential solution into the conflicts and challenges of civic society and the whole human race (cf. *LG* 28).

One cannot and must not demand of the faithful and not even of all the clergy that they acquire a detailed knowledge of biblical exegesis and the latest research in the field of theology and the history of dogma. But everyone can without any difficulty find out what the Church teaches authoritatively about the Sacrament of Holy Orders. It can be found in the Roman Catechism (1566), which stresses the Tridentine ideal of the priest as a preacher of the word of God and shepherd of the community (*Cat. Rom.* Part II, Chap. 7).

The *Catechism of the Catholic Church* (English translation 1994) contains a concise rendering of Vatican II's teaching on the Sacrament of Holy Orders (Part 2, Section 2, Chap. 3, Art. 6). With divine and Catholic faith the Church therefore professes: "Holy Orders is the sacrament through which the mission entrusted by Christ to his apostles continues to be exercised in the Church until the end of time: thus it is the sacrament of apostolic ministry. It includes three degrees: episcopate, presbyterate, and diaconate" (*CCC* 1536).

9.

THE SPIRITUAL LIFE AND PASTORAL WORK OF THE PRIEST

Dear Confreres and Fellow Christians,

Now that we have considered the origin of the priesthood in Christ and how it took shape in the apostolic Church by looking at sacred scripture and the testimonies of the Church Fathers, we can gather all the individual aspects into one perspective. The biblical witness is far from offering us a plurality of images of the Church and models of ecclesial office that are as impossible to integrate as would seem to be the case at first sight. It is only when the Church is torn apart into an invisible community of grace, which manifests itself in the present in preaching, Baptism, and the Lord's Supper, and a visible gathering of enrolled members, who are organized according to contemporary sociological and political models, that the New Testament appears to justify an arbitrary reshaping of the one "office" to suit one's needs and the respective power constellation.

Jesus chose some of his disciples and gave them a share in his messianic consecration and sending by the Father. After Easter, in the Church that had resulted from Pentecost, the apostolate emerged as the main foundation of the visible and sacramental Church. The activity of the apostles in building up the Church can be summed up under three categories of ministry, namely teaching, governing, and sanctifying; these are nonetheless

135

united and identical in being rooted in the mission and authority
they received from Christ. They comprise evangelists, prophets,
teachers, shepherds, fishers of men, laborers in the vineyard, and
soldiers who suffer for Christ in his militia and fight with spiritual
weapons against evil (cf. 1 Cor 9:7; 2 Tim 2:3; 4,7; Eph 6:10–
17). The apostles are plowmen in God's fields and threshers of
his crops (cf. 1 Cor 9:10), or they are master builders of God's
house (*oikos*) and temple (cf. 1 Cor 3:10) and stewards (*oikonomoi*)
of God's mysteries (1 Cor 4:1). These are the same people in the
one apostolic mission, whether the name of their direct activity
is used to describe them, for example, teacher, or whether images
are borrowed from architecture or from agriculture and livestock
breeding (e.g., the relationship of pastor and flock). A fixed terminology then develops for the shepherds of the Church and
teachers of the gospel deployed in the apostolic communities:
sometimes the name of their status as leaders, overseers, and
presbyters is used and sometimes the noun denoting the office is
derived from their activity of *episkopein* or *diakonein*. The place of
the itinerant "apostles, . . . prophets . . . and teachers" (cf. Eph
4:11; *Did.* 11,1.3; 15,1) who go from community to community
as "your high priests" (*Did.* 13,3) is taken locally by the "bishops
and deacons" (Phil 1:1; *Did.* 15,1).

The whole development is linked together in the faith understanding that the Catholic Church consists in and from the local
churches. For the individual local churches, the principle of
their unity with the apostolic origin of the current community
of all its shepherds and faithful is embodied in the bishop; the
presbyterium and the deacons, on the other hand, represent
the principle of plurality in the community of the overseers
and servants and all the faithful of the diocese, the *episkope*. To
different degrees the bishops, priests, and deacons all share in
Christ's authority and mission, both of which he conferred on
the apostles to the end of the age (cf. Mt 28:20). In this way,
they also fulfill the central commission given to the apostles,
namely to teach, govern, and sanctify the People of God. As
all the members of the Body of Christ work together and in

so doing build it up in love, the bishops, priests, and deacons of the Church, "which is his body" (Eph 1:23), are given by Christ (cf. Eph 4:11) in order "to equip the saints for the work of ministry, for building up the body of Christ, until all of us come to the unity of the faith and of the knowledge of the Son of God, to maturity, to the measure of the full stature of Christ" (Eph 4:12f.).

In other words, the responsibility of all Christians for the life and mission of the Church is also expressed here. It is what is elsewhere called the common priesthood of all the faithful and the ministerial priesthood of the servants of Christ and the Church.

Hence it seems to me to be appropriate to:

1. consider the root and foundation (*Wurzelgrund*) of the priesthood in the Trinity, the Incarnation, and the sending of the Holy Spirit;
2. portray its three functions of teaching, governing, and sanctifying; and
3. comment on its inner and outer way of life, that is, its unity with the triune God in prayer, discipleship of Christ, and attitude of mind.

The divine Trinity is the source and origin of creation and self-communication as the truth and life of mankind. "Thus, the Church has been seen as 'a people made one with the unity of the Father, the Son and the Holy Spirit'" (*LG* 4).

Consequently we do not force the multifarious statements of scripture, the apostolic tradition, and the Church's magisterium into one subjective schema and become slaves of the constraints of a particular thought system when we unfold the essence of the Catholic priesthood from its foundation in God's trinitarian self-revelation. The eternal and incarnate Word of God, the Son of the Father, the crucified and risen Lord, gives his disciples a share in his mission from the Father. Catholic theology does not create systems in the way idealist philosophy does; rather, it develops from the *analogia fidei*, the intimate referential connectedness of revelation (*nexus mysteriorum*), an insight that does not seize hold of the mystery but allows itself to be illuminated by its light. Jesus communicates to them the Spirit in whom he and the Father are eternally one and which anoints and permeates the humanity he took on at the Incarnation, so that he is recognized as the Messiah and Savior of the whole world. "'As the Father has sent me, so I send you.' When he had said this, he breathed on them and said to them, 'Receive the Holy Spirit'" (Jn 20:21f.).

The bishops and presbyters who were instituted by the apostles through imposition of hands and prayer in every community as their coworkers and successors (cf. Acts 14:23) shepherd the Church of God, which he won for himself through Christ's salvific deed. Furthermore, they are appointed by the Holy Spirit (cf. Acts 20:28). The trinitarian ultimate ground of Christ's person and mission had already been revealed at his baptism in the Jordan (cf. Lk 3:21f.).

So we are coworkers of God, servants of Jesus Christ, and missionaries of the Holy Spirit.

Coworkers of God—*Cooperatores Veritatis*

"For we are God's servants, working together; you are God's field, God's building" (1 Cor 3:9; cf. 2 Cor 6:1), we are "co-workers with the truth" (3 Jn 1:8). This is analogous to what the Lord said to the apostles and the 72 disciples: "The harvest is plentiful, but the labourers are few; therefore ask the Lord of the harvest to send out labourers into his harvest" (Lk 10:2).

God realized his universal plan of salvation in Christ and this was to be made known to all through the Church (cf. Eph 3:10). The apostle and the Church were "to bring to the Gentiles the news of the boundless riches of Christ, and to make everyone see what is the plan of the mystery hidden for ages in God who created all things" (Eph 3:8f.). But in order that all people should come to know God, to place their hope in him in life and death, and to be filled with the Holy Spirit in their love of God and neighbor, it is necessary for people to be coworkers in his service.

The priest is a true *co-operator Dei*. The apostle builds up the house of God and serves the Church with "the gift of God's grace that was given to me by the working of his power" (Eph 3:7). Of course, God has no need of our help in order to realize and complete his work. But it belongs to man's freedom and dignity that God gives him the grace to collaborate in his own salvation and that of others. Although we can do nothing without God (cf. Jn 15:5), with his help we can "do greater works" (Jn 14:12), not in order to relieve God of some of the bother he has with us but rather to glorify him.

For it is God's joy to see that we are there for one another, both in the practical necessities of our earthly existence and in sharing together in looking after our eternal salvation. Those who have come to faith through preaching are introduced into the mystery of Christ in Baptism and Confirmation. And the apex and apogee of their initiation is spiritual communion with the Son's sacrificial giving of himself to the Father and sacramental communion with him in the Eucharist. When the priest sees the multiplication of thanksgiving to God in the participation of many in the Eucharist and the glory of God being revealed in the living believer, then he is filled with awe at the glorious nature of his ministry in the Spirit who gives life (cf. 2 Cor 3:6) because "we are workers with you for your joy" (2 Cor 1:24).

Revelation is not a psychodrama but rather a world event. The task of the Protestant predicant would confine itself to testifying to faith as trust in justification for Christ's sake. In the Catholic understanding, in his preaching and in the sacraments, the priest truly participates instrumentally and causally in mediating the salvation through which we are "called children of God; and that is what we are" (1 Jn 3:1). In the Sacrament of Holy Orders the priest is endowed with the sacred power (*sacra*

potestas) "of consecrating and offering the true Body and Blood
of the Lord and of remitting and retaining sins" (DH 1771), and
the bishop additionally with "the power to confirm and ordain"
(DH 1777). There is a great difference between the sacraments
working because they are believed in and working because in
them Christ really communicates justifying and sanctifying grace
through the priest, whom he uses like a living instrument as a
"steward of God's mysteries" (1 Cor 4:1). On account of the
Sacrament of Holy Orders, the priesthood differs essentially
from "only the office (*officium*) and bare ministry of preaching
the gospel" (DH 1771).

Through our new being in Christ, we are also enabled
through sanctifying grace to perform meritorious acts as far
as finally achieving salvation in heaven is concerned. We are
likewise made capable of using our powers to share in bringing about the salvation of the world. Theocentricity mediated through Christocentricity grounded in the Incarnation also
includes responsibility for the world in the family, in the work-
place, in culture, and in politics, inasmuch as the "good works"
are meritorious and relevant to salvation (cf. *GS* 33–39). For the
redeemed world and the world to be redeemed are also part of
the glorification of God. All the good that we do in our words
and works serves to glorify God and consolidates the experience
of redemption.

The Enlightenment and the criticism of religion in the eighteenth and nineteenth centuries, as well as their ideological after-
effects in the twentieth century, produced a crude caricature of
Christianity in narrowing it down to salvation in an (imaginary)
afterlife, which it rejected, and demanding instead that man
should take charge of this world as the sphere and locus of his
self-redemption. But man has the same God to thank for his
nature and grace, the God who is his Creator, Redeemer, and
Reconciler. In the penultimate state of the world, God is already
glorified when the intellectual and material creativity of human
reason places itself in the service of a progressive improvement
and humanization of all conditions of life. The eternal does not

invalidate time; for God's Son became man in order to raise and perfect us human beings and the whole of creation in him. In his collaboration, man does not supplement God's work; rather, he is challenged to allow God's work to come to full fruition in him as the planted vine takes root in us and finally bears rich fruit. What is meant here is, of course, not Christ's unique and complete work of salvation to which nothing needs to be added but rather its being made present, being accepted, and bearing fruit in the life of the individual, in the community of disciples, and in the whole of humanity when the members of the Body of Christ "grow up in every way into him who is the head, into Christ" (Eph 4:15) and "all things are subjected to him [. . .], so that God may be all in all" (1 Cor 15:28).

Winning people for Christ, accompanying them on their journey of discipleship of Christ, and justifying oneself to everyone who asks about the *Sinngrund* (basis of meaning), the Logos, of our hope (cf. 1 Pt 3:15)—all this brings with it a great deal of effort, hardship, and even disappointment. But this ministry also fills us with joy when we can assure young parents that their children are called to eternal life and that in Baptism they are freed from the power of sin and "transferred [. . .] into the kingdom of his beloved Son" (Col 1:13).

In a society in which God seems to many people to be an illusion that was unmasked by the Enlightenment and science, the priest is not respected as a man of God but rather derided as a holy joker (*Himmelskomiker*) or even opposed as a deceived deceiver. Several tens of thousands of Catholic and Orthodox priests as well as Protestant pastors were exterminated like vermin as enemies of progress and science in the persecutions carried out in the French and Russian Revolutions, in the struggle against the Freemasons in Mexico, and by the Communists in Spain and the Nazis in occupied Europe. But the priest as a witness to God's truth and thus an adversary of the political and religious programs of self-redemption is for that very reason at all times exposed to verbal and physical hostility. However, the words the apostle addressed to Timothy in the first Christian century also apply to us priests today: "Do not be ashamed, then, of the testimony about our Lord [. . .], but join with me in suffering for the gospel, relying on the power of God" (2 Tim 1:8).

We can only escape "the drama of atheist humanism" as found in Marx, Engels, Comte, and Nietzsche, and described so harrowingly by Henri de Lubac in the middle of the Second World War and at the height of the Holocaust,[14] through a new humanism which performs the whole drama of human existence in the world and in history in the light of "the goodness and loving-kindness of God" (Ti 3:4) and plays it through until our "renewal by the Holy Spirit" (Ti 3:5). Western atheism is at heart a protest against the social dominance of one Christian denomination in a state, an intellectual and political dominance justified metaphysically and theologically with God and revelation. God as the pillar of an unjust social order, a morality demanding too much of real people, and a view of history long since overtaken by natural and historical science as well as an anthropology differing in its starting point from that of the human sciences—all these are what atheism, agnosticism, and critical philosophy regard as their declared enemy. Only doing without metaphysics and church dogmatics would, they argue, guarantee a pluralist, liberal, and tolerant fundamental attitude as the basis for a progressive and science-friendly body politic. Only if religion were declared to be a private matter and the Church banished to a subculture, could the catastrophes of wars of religion and ideology be avoided. This intellectual conflict situation, which came to be shared by many intellectuals and also gripped broad levels of society in a popularized fashion, is something the priest nowadays has to reckon with in the social media, schools, and universities as well as in private conversation, even extending into Catholic parishes. There the tension is painfully felt between the Creed and the seeming evidence from the intellectual and cultural history of the last three centuries. When he starts, every new bishop and priest is tested with a list of questions to establish whether he is conservative or liberal.

This then constitutes a burden of prejudices that impede and obstruct direct access to the word of God and to the Church's teaching on faith and morals. We must make it very clear that God is not the stopgap for an antiquated system of explaining the world, let alone the pillar propping up inherited weaknesses and evils in intellectual, cultural, and social life.

By showing itself sensitive to the difficulties with faith and the collective prejudices of many people in the present day, the Second Vatican Council chooses an anthropological approach to supernatural faith. This must not, however, be confused with reducing theology to anthropology. In spite of all the social change and progress in science and technology, the fundamental existential questions that all humanity shares in every age remain: "[W]hat is man? What is this sense of sorrow, of evil, of death, which continues to exist despite so much progress? What purpose have these victories purchased at so high a cost? What can man offer to society, what can he expect from it? What follows this earthly life?" (*GS* 10).

By going into these questions the Church shows that she takes people seriously and accepts them. But she is not the one who could answer them. For she herself is also only made up of human beings who share these existential challenges with others. But the Church bears witness to the self-revelation of God, who displayed his solidarity with us in the suffering and death of Jesus. In his Resurrection from the dead we have been given the promise of life and granted the light and strength to be able to pursue our vocation.

And the following defines the Church's position in today's world: "Hence under the light of Christ, the image of the unseen God, the firstborn of every creature, the council wishes to speak to all men in order to shed light on the mystery of man and to cooperate in finding the solution to the outstanding problems of our time" (*GS* 10).

The priest is a "man of God" who must "Fight the good fight of the faith" (1 Tim 6:11f.). We belong to the pilgrim Church, which does not stroll peacefully and cosily through history and,

like a Platonic community of ideas, remain untouched by conflicts with the world. Like Jesus, "who in his testimony before
Pontius Pilate made the good confession" witnessing to the truth
(1 Tim 6:13; cf. Jn 18:36f.), the priest, too, should be affected
by the "joys and the hopes, the griefs and the anxieties of the
men of this age" (*GS* 1). As long as we have not yet reached our
heavenly home, the priest stands in the midst of the suffering
and struggling Church: "By the power of the risen Lord it [the
Church] is given strength that it might, in patience and in love,
overcome its sorrows and its challenges, both within itself and
from without, and that it might reveal to the world, faithfully
though darkly, the mystery of its Lord until, in the end, it will
be manifested in full light" (*LG* 8).

SERVANTS OF CHRIST AND STEWARDS OF GOD'S MYSTERIES

The Eternal Word, who is God, proceeds eternally from the
Father. And the Son is sent into the world by the Father in order
to carry out his plan of salvation so that all mankind should
come to know the truth. In the Incarnation, the unity is revealed
between the eternal procession of the Son from the Father and
the sending of Christ within time. This being sent into the world
and remaining with the Church until the end of time is transferred by Christ himself to the disciples. The disciples continued
the task of salvation in the power of the Holy Spirit from the
Father and the Son. In his name, they taught the people to keep
all that Jesus had commanded and mediated sacramentally the
reconciliation that had been brought about once and for all, so
that through being baptized in the name of the Father and the
Son and the Holy Spirit, the believer becomes a son or daughter
of God and can, through the Son in the Holy Spirit, call God
Abba, Father. St. Paul understands himself and his coworkers
in the apostolate "as servants of Christ and stewards of God's
mysteries" (1 Cor 4:1). The apostles are assigned the office of

reconciliation. In God's place and in the person of Christ they ask the faithful to allow the reconciliation of the world with God through Christ to take effect in their lives.

Thus the apostles, bishops, and priests are in a singular sense "servants of the word" (Lk 1:2). The priest "must have a firm grasp of the word that is trustworthy in accordance with the teaching" (Ti 1:9). They are servants of the new covenant who, in the person of Christ, the high priest of the new and eternal covenant, teach the people with the gospel of Christ. They lead the Church as good shepherds. They sanctify the faithful through baptism in the name of the triune God (cf. Mt 28:19), confirmation with the Holy Spirit (cf. Acts 8:17), the celebration of the eucharistic sacrifice (cf. 1 Cor 11:25; Acts 20:7), the forgiveness of sins committed after baptism (cf. 2 Cor 5:20), anointing the sick (Jas 5:14), ordaining new stewards of the mysteries in sacred ordination (cf. 1 Tim 5:22; Ti 1:5; Acts 14:23), and blessing marriages so that they might take place "only in the Lord" (1 Cor 7:39). Combined with this is the individual pastoral care of offering words of encouragement, advice, and comfort to both the sorrowing and the joyful, the young, and the dying within the whole compass of spiritual, intellectual, and physical works of compassion and mercy.

Jesus came to proclaim the kingdom of God and to bring it. He preached repentance and belief in the gospel, which he is in his person. This gospel comprises his destiny right down to his dying on the Cross for the forgiveness of sins, his Resurrection from the dead, his remaining with us in the Holy Spirit, his efficacy through the Church until the end of time, and his coming again. Being a servant of Christ is thus identical with being a servant of the gospel.

Jesus allowed the twelve apostles and the 72 disciples to share in a special way in his consecration as Messiah and his sending by the Father. The Messiah is the Christ, the Lord's anointed by the Holy Spirit (cf. Jn 1:41). Priests do not baptize and forgive sins in the name of the parish and with its authority, but in the name of Christ, the head of the Church. The basis of the authority of the bishops and priests is trinitarian, Christological, and pneumatological, but it is also linked ecclesiologically with the current charisms of the rest of the faithful in a community of action. "Now there are varieties of gifts (*charismata*), but the same Spirit; and there are varieties of services (*diakoniai*), but the same Lord; and there are varieties of activities (*energematai*), but it is the same God who activates all of them in everyone. [. . .] Are all apostles? Are all prophets? Are all teachers?" (1 Cor 12:4–6, 29).

In his Incarnation, the Word took up the whole of humanity into his human nature, taking on the sin of the world and rendering it harmless so that through faith we become children of God in him. "Whoever believes in the Son has eternal life; whoever disobeys the Son will not see life, but must endure God's wrath" (Jn 3:36). The community of the faithful is connected to the Incarnate Word in the same way as the body is to the head. The Church is the fellowship of the faithful, who have fellowship with the Father in the Son (cf. 1 Jn 1:3). She is bound to Jesus as the bride is to the bridegroom. The Messiah, the Word become flesh (cf. Jn 1:14), is the bridegroom of his Church (cf. Jn 3:29; Eph 5:32). The apostle's relationship with his community is not like the impersonal relationship of an employee with his firm. He loves the faithful "with divine jealousy" (2 Cor 11:2). It is the love of Christ that drives him, so that he can say to the faithful in Corinth: "I promised you in marriage to one husband, to present you as a chaste virgin to Christ" (2 Cor 11:2). The priest represents Jesus in a sacramental way as the head and bridegroom of the Church in that Christ himself works salvation by teaching, governing, and sanctifying through him. But he is not the head and bridegroom in the proper sense. He will follow the example of John the Baptist in humbly pointing away from himself to the Lord because he is merely the "friend of the bridegroom, who [. . .] rejoices greatly at the bridegroom's voice" (Jn 3:29).

When he sees that the individual soul and the whole Church enter into a bond in the faith and the love of Christ like that between bride and bridegroom, he can then say with John the

Baptist that he has heard the bridegroom's voice and "For this reason my joy has been fulfilled" (Jn 3:29).

The innermost spirituality of the Catholic priest lies in his being able to say, with the true priest whom he serves in mind, "He must increase, but I must decrease" (Jn 3:30).

But if bishop and priest represent Christ as the head and bridegroom of his Church, then this cannot be just a functionalist representation in the way that a president represents a state, an NGO, or a club.

Through consecration and the imparting of the Holy Spirit, the person thus consecrated to God and the service of Christ is inwardly conformed or configured to Christ, the shepherd and bridegroom of his Church. The priest is an icon and *Imago Christi*. His image is imprinted forever in the soul of the person ordained (*character indelebilis*). This character remains indelible even though the spiritual authority bestowed is no longer exercised in heaven since there is no longer any need there to administer the sacraments.

In the Sacrament of Holy Orders "priests, by the anointing of the Holy Spirit, are signed with a special character and are conformed to Christ the Priest in such a way that they can act in the person of Christ the Head" (*PO* 2). The reason for the Sacraments of Baptism, Confirmation, and Holy Orders being permitted to be administered only once is not based on a positive stipulation in human canon law or an ancient custom. Rather, the person baptized is reborn in Christ and incorporated into his Body, so that he is one body with the Lord. A person who is ordained accomplishes nothing out of his own sanctity and with his own merits and cannot frustrate God's salvific will even when these are lacking. Instead, he is so indissolubly linked to the person of the head of the Church (*res et sacramentum*) that Christ himself teaches, governs, and sanctifies through him.

The Council of Trent states: "If anyone says that by sacred ordination the Holy Spirit is not given and that, therefore, the bishops say in vain: 'Receive the Holy Spirit'; or if he says that no character is imprinted by ordination; or that he who has once been a priest can again become a layman, let him be anathema" (DH 1774).

The opinion that the doctrine of the lasting effect of ordination with the imprinting of an indelible seal was "invented" by St. Augustine as an argument against the Donatists is an absurdity from the point of view of both the history of dogmatics and systematic theology. For the person ordained is completely filled with the promise of grace and the transferral to him of being sent by the Father. But this relationship to Christ cannot remain external to the person being sent; otherwise it would be Christ's messenger in all his human weakness and fickleness on whom man's salvation depended. In order that his divine salvation should not depend on his human servants, Christ made the apostles his servants and instruments who did not themselves bring about salvation but merely mediated it effectively in the sacraments.

Only in this way is it possible to appreciate what it means when the Lord says: "Whoever listens to you listens to me" (Lk 10:16). Paul writes to the doubting Corinthians: "[S]ince you desire proof that *Christ is speaking in me.* He is not weak in dealing with you, but is powerful in you" (2 Cor 13:3, italics mine). The apostles are as inseparably linked to Jesus as the voice is to the Word that has become flesh. The sense of superiority of priests over the "laity" that was to be found in medieval society up to the Reformation rested secondarily on the education gap between them and has no theological justification. For the office of priest is not conferred in order to satisfy ambition and vanity, but rather so that a person should be conformed to Christ's humility and serve the salvation of all people.

The priest is the image of Christ. Hence there cannot legitimately be different, let alone opposing, images of the priest. In an age of relativism, according to which *the* truth is said not to exist and everyone can therefore concoct his or her own truth, this statement sounds eminently seasonable and has the evidence of this mutable paradigm on its side.

But "Jesus Christ is the same yesterday and today and for ever" (Heb 13:8). All priests are teachers and shepherds in the image of Christ. And in this they are all high priests of the new covenant and together, under the leadership of the bishop, form a *communio* in the presbytery. This does not, however, result in uniformity in the way that the individuality of functionaries is ground down until they are interchangeable. In the Catholic faith, the principles of unity and pluriformity are conveyed in a different way, which means that any socially incompetent individualism and a collectivism that destroys the person's uniqueness are excluded from the start.

When he chooses the apostles, we see how Jesus calls each one by name and how different they are in character as well as in their occupations, which also shape their mentalities differently. That is why there is not just one model for them either. For all of them the task is to win people for Christ with apostolic zeal and to teach, govern, and sanctify them in the name of Jesus.

10.

THE PRIEST IN THE MARTYRIA, LEITURGIA, AND DIAKONIA OF THE CHURCH

Dear Confreres and Fellow Christians,

All the various natural gifts and inclinations are a benefit for the corporate good of the Church. Although most priests are pastors of a parish, others are needed to take on the pastoral care of specific spheres of life and social groups. It is the most responsible task of a bishop or a religious superior to achieve a balance between the *bonum commune ecclesiae* and the various gifts and charisms of his priests and deacons. We need committed and competent ministers in the parishes, in prisons and military chaplaincies, in hospitals and retirement homes, in schools and universities; and the bishop must encourage and enable his priests to undergo the appropriate advanced training for this. He also has to make sure that gifted young priests are prepared in the sacred sciences so as to be able to use them one day in the service of mankind in its search for truth and of the Church in her proclamation of the gospel (cf. *LG* 25).

An anti-intellectual retreat into "purely giving pastoral care to ordinary people" and disparaging theology professors as "scribes and pharisees" who are blind to reality would do great harm to the Church. For faith and reason both come from God as their sole source. We would be playing into the hands of those who dismiss faith as "non-knowledge" or as a subjective option that cannot be mediated through arguments. The Catholic priest in particular—from curate to cardinal and from parish priest to professor—must "Always be ready to make your defense to anyone who demands from you an account of the hope that is in you" (1 Pt 3:15).

IN THE POWER OF THE HOLY SPIRIT

The procession of the person of the Holy Spirit from the Father and the Son in the Trinity is what underlies the sending of the Holy Spirit into the world. The sending of the Son for the salvation of the world in our flesh (cf. Jn 1:14; Rom 8:3; Gal 4:4; Heb 2:14) constitutes the culmination of the salvation history that will be made unsurpassably manifest in the outpouring of the Holy Spirit over all flesh, the Church, and the apostles in the last days (cf. Acts 2:1–47, esp. 17–21).

Paul sums up the mysteries of the Trinity, the Incarnation, grace, and the Church with unparalleled clarity when he professes: "But when the fullness of time had come, God sent his Son, born of a woman, [. . .] so that we might receive adoption as children. And because you are children, God has sent the Spirit of his Son into our hearts, crying, 'Abba! Father!'" (Gal 4:4–6).

Already at Jesus' baptism in the Jordan it is evident that the human nature he took on in the Incarnation is anointed by the Holy Spirit and thus permeated and guided by this Spirit. On the Cross he breathes out his spirit and in so doing creates man's life anew. In Baptism we become a new creation. In the power of the Spirit, Jesus carries out his work of salvation to its conclusion, to the Cross; in the power of the Spirit, the Father raised him from the dead.

It is the Spirit of the Messiah that the Lord bestows on his apostles: "Receive the Holy Spirit" (Jn 20:22). In the Holy Spirit they share in his mission from the Father. They can forgive the sins of the penitent and retain the sins of the obdurate. It remains true that only God can forgive sins, but Jesus' words also confirm that he has given the disciples the (instrumental) authority to forgive sins in the Sacraments of Baptism, Reconciliation, and the Anointing of the Sick if the recipient opens him- or herself to God's grace in faith and love and freely accepts it.

So it is also the Holy Spirit who makes bishops and presbyters shepherds in God's Church (cf. Acts 20:28) through the laying on of hands and the effective consecratory prayer. Timothy, as the prototype of the successors of the apostles and thus of bishops and presbyters (cf. 1 Tim 5:22), received the grace of the Holy Spirit through the imposition of hands and the consecratory prayer of the apostle with the presbytery (cf. 1 Tim 4:14; 2 Tim 1:6).

In the power of the Holy Spirit, the bishop guards "the good treasure entrusted to you" (2 Tim 1:14) of the true faith and the sound teaching of the Church, which goes back to the teaching of Christ and the teaching of the apostles and contains them both. The Spirit that is given here in order to lead "the church of the living God, the pillar and bulwark of the truth" (1 Tim 3:15) is not an ad hoc charism but rather a sacramental grace that enables its recipients to teach in the name of Christ and to govern God's Church. The Holy Spirit conforms the ordained to Christ, so that the priest governs and sanctifies the Church in the person of the head of the Church. But this grace nevertheless serves the recipient's own personal sanctification less than the other sacraments do; instead, it enables him to sanctify his fellow Christians.

But the Holy Spirit, who gives the spiritual authority imparted its efficacy, is also the source and measure of the priest's spiritual attitude. Priestly spirituality has nothing to do with pious sentiments and being romantically taken with one's own importance. We have received a Spirit that overcomes our faintheartedness and our cowardice before the "enemy," that is, the seemingly superior power of evil. For God gave us "a spirit of power and of love and of self-discipline" (2 Tim 1:7). The Spirit of God gives us priests the equilibrium and inner calm we need in volatile situations, too. "And the Lord's servant must not be quarrelsome but kindly to everyone, an apt teacher, patient, correcting opponents with gentleness. God may perhaps grant that they will repent and come to know the truth, and that they may escape from the snare of the devil, having been held captive by him to do his will" (2 Tim 2:24–26).

In accordance with the Council's teaching, "Bishops, therefore, with their helpers, the priests and deacons, have taken up the service of the community, presiding in place of God over the flock, whose shepherds they are, as teachers for doctrine, priests for sacred worship, and ministers for governing" (*LG* 20). This corresponds to the three basic functions of the Church: *martyria*, *leiturgia*, and *diakonia*.

TEACHERS FOR DOCTRINE

One of the principal duties of bishops and priests is the preaching of the gospel (cf. *LG* 25) or the ministry of the word (cf. *PO* 4). This takes the form of homily and catechesis, preaching, talks, and written testimonies.

The risen Lord sends the apostles out into the world so that they themselves and in their successors should teach all people everything he has commanded them (cf. Mt 28:19f.).

Since faith comes from hearing and without it no one can find salvation, the first of the three sacred duties (*munera*) is the proclamation of the gospel or the teaching of our faith. To be sure, only God can infuse faith in people's hearts. Jesus is the true inner teacher, who effectively speaks the word of salvation to us. But because man is a physical, historical being with an intellect that is passive and receptive (*intellectus possibilis*), the message must enter into the individual via his outer senses so that he can assess what he has heard with his active or agent intellect (*intellectus agens*). It is with his will that he then decides whether to obey the word of God and follow its instructions in freedom. Only when the Holy Spirit infuses the divine virtues into our hearts does the human act of faith bring salvation, allow us to share in the knowledge of God, and lead us to be united with God in love. In faith we know God. In hope we approach him as our goal. In love we unite ourselves with him now and in all eternity. Man is a natural being, but one directed towards God's revelation in his intellect and freedom. Faith is the divine fire that lights the wick of the candle if it meets with approval in the free will. Obedience to God is the supreme realization of freedom, taking the form of man's unity with God in love. That is why faith comes about when supernatural grace and the Church's proclamation work together. The apostles give thanks to God that the Thessalonians have accepted the word they preached not just as a human word about an idea or a system of thought but rather as what it really is, namely, "God's word, which is also at work in you believers" (1 Thess 2:13).

The words of the prophet can also be well applied to the ministers of the word in the new covenant: "For the lips of a priest should guard knowledge, and people should seek instruction from his mouth, for he is the messenger of the Lord of hosts" (Mal 2:7).

Since what the word contains is God's supernatural self-revelation, its truth cannot be known, and freely acknowledged, by reason unless this is accompanied by grace.

Since the Enlightenment, the possibility of a supernatural knowledge of God, indeed the very existence of God, has been disputed in many philosophical systems, especially by empiricism, materialism, and positivism. Skepticism and agnosticism doubt and deny the knowability of the truth and thus the existence of God.

Moreover, relativism disputes the capacity for truth of "weak reason" altogether. The conclusions that are drawn from the concept of "weak reason" are paradoxical: absolute truth is claimed for empirical and practical knowledge, whereas insights into natural moral law or the cognition of revealed truth are relativized. If biblical revelation or the historical religions are to have any epistemic significance or moral use at all, then this is merely as a culturally determined code for fundamental existential questions. They serve to overcome contingency or form the moral corset for secular societies. The Christian faith's conviction of the objective truth of its Creed and of the events of salvation history is suspect as dogmatism that is said ultimately to result from a claim to power on the part of the Church as an institution which cannot be legitimized. Based on these premises, the Church would appear to be the adversary of freedom and self-determination when she adheres to objective norms and the general validity of natural moral law.

This climate of relativism makes the priests' service of the word of truth more difficult and tempts them to take the easier path of conforming to the prevailing ideological norms and paradigms. The Church should, so the argument goes, be made fit for today's society by "rethinking" those ethical norms and truths of the faith that are out of touch with the world and no longer "communicable."

But in the Christian faith truth does not present itself as a system of dogmas, scientific theses, and moral postulates. The truth is God himself, who has revealed himself as the Way, the Truth, and the Life in Jesus Christ, his Word, which took on our flesh.

What Jesus once pointed out to Pilate in his praetorium, the judgment hall of secular pragmatic reason with its power over life and death, is something that occurs over and over again: power is confused with truth. But they are two quite different things, power and truth. Power cannot compel truth, and truth will not bow to power alone. God's power and kingship do not coerce in the imperial sense of *parcere subiectis et debellare superbos* but rather set people free for "the freedom of the glory of the children of God" (Rom 8:21). Jesus' servants do not fight with the sword. The "good soldier of Christ Jesus" (2 Tim 2:2) suffers with and for the Lord, so that faith in Christ can profess him in complete freedom.

In this spirit, Jesus reveals before the potentates of this world the mystery of his person and mission as the true ruler who has overcome the world and now brings truth and freedom. Jesus answered Pilate: "You say that I am a king. For this I was born, and for this I came into the world, to testify to the truth. Everyone who belongs to the truth listens to my voice" (Jn 18:37). Pilate is irritated and can only snarl back at him the skeptic's defiant cry of "What is truth?" (Jn 18:38).

In their discipleship of Jesus those who serve God's word are reminded to "Do your best to present yourself to God as one approved by him, a worker who has no need to be ashamed, rightly explaining the word of truth" (2 Tim 2:15). When we profess Jesus Christ, who is the Truth in person, all the truths of the faith and the Church's teaching are contained and united in this profession.

The style in which the faith is taught is determined by the content of what is taught: a profession of God, his Son, and the Holy Spirit together with all the salvific deeds of creation, salvation, and perfection.

It is not a matter of knowledge content being drummed into people and mechanically drilled. The important thing is to awaken a love for Jesus that leads to a true knowledge of God as well as a correct assessment of one's own existence within the overall context of the world and history. The apostle did not come to give brilliant speeches to an illustrious audience that delighted in them.

The motto of a kind and patient teacher and honest witness to God must be: "My speech and my proclamation were not with plausible words of wisdom, but with a demonstration of the Spirit and of power, so that your faith might rest not on human wisdom but on the power of God" (1 Cor 2:4f.).

A recent issue within the Church is the disastrous pitting against one another of doctrine and praxis, orthodoxy and orthopraxis. But theologically, doctrine does not mean an edifice of ideas or a theoretical exploration of the world as it does in idealism; nor is it the verification of a program in practice as is the case in materialism. The Marxist philosophers suddenly wanted not only to interpret the world but even to change it. In view of the havoc they wrought, one feels like replying with a sigh: "If only they had let it be!"

God reveals himself in his word, in which he is recognized, and in his action, in which he sets us free. The Christian glorifies God in words and deeds. In Christ the truth is at the same time life, knowledge, and renewal. Just as it is impossible to separate the divine and the human natures in Christ, it is equally impossible to tear apart his mission as a teacher and as a shepherd. Christian dogmatics is not an obstacle to pastoral praxis since it does not reflect our thinking about God but rather what God says about us. And Christian praxis does not mean self-redemption but rather the hope that makes us capable of loving our neighbor and taking responsibility for the world. We do not need any class warfare in the Church but rather to overcome it in true fraternal community.

How can the faith be taught and the word preached in a culture whose ideal is the well-informed and mature citizen? Does a highly educated thinker, a specialist in his subject, someone who holds a position of responsibility in politics, culture, or jurisprudence have to allow himself to be told what to do by a preacher with a mediocre education?

Priests as servants of the word do in fact benefit from a broad general education and a good knowledge of modern developments in digitalization, globalization, etc. But with the complexity and profusion of fields of knowledge, even the most gifted of people quickly find themselves stretched to their limits. Nor can an above-average IQ be the decisive criterion for a pastoral ministry that consists in the dedication and willingness to make sacrifices of a good shepherd for his sheep.

The priest's task in his proclamation is not to engage in a theoretical disputation with philosophy and the sciences, as is the case in academic theology, but rather to bear witness to Christ as man's truth and life. He is a preacher of the faith, albeit in a well-reflected form. And the hearer should be strengthened in his or her faith through the words that are preached, not play the censor. Where knowledge is not humbly placed at the service of the common good, it puffs itself up, playing with fire with its vanities and provoking unnecessary wrangling. Humility is a question of character and is to be found in both intellectuals and artisans. The "little children" (as opposed to "the learned and the clever") (Lk 10:21, NJB) do not hesitate to admit that all our wisdom does not come from us but from God. And it is in them that the unity of Father and Son in their divine being has been made known as well as in God's self-revelation.

To fellows who prided themselves on their reason and thought they could free themselves from the lifelong sequence of learning and teaching, wanting only to be teachers, Bernard of Clairvaux already said: "He that will teach himself in school, becomes a scholar to a fool" (*Ep.* 87,7).

But the priest, too, must mark these words so that he does not teach on his own authority. He must above all constantly learn from the word of God in scripture and tradition. Only those who have heard the word of God and like Mary treasured and pondered it in their hearts (cf. Lk 2:19) will be "kindly to everyone, an apt teacher, patient" (2 Tim 2:24.). If there is a temptation among laity and priests to deny each other's competence and to sow discord in the parishes, they should together learn this lesson in the school of Christ: "Nor must you allow yourselves to be called teachers, for you have only one Teacher, the Christ. The greatest among you must be your servant. Anyone who raises himself up *will* be humbled, and anyone who humbles himself *will* be raised up" (Mt 23:10–12, NJB, italics mine).

PRIESTS FOR SACRED WORSHIP

The "priestly" is a category with which the Church describes her ministry of sanctifying mankind, that is, of continually infusing man's physical and spiritual life with God's Spirit and truth. When man's whole relationship to God is portrayed in visible signs, we call this "lifting hearts to God" the sacred liturgy. The *leiturgia* is not the sum total of the Church's mission, but it does constitute the integrating focus of *martyria* and *diakonia*, of proc-lamation and responsibility for the world. "Nevertheless the liturgy is the summit toward which the activity of the Church is directed; at the same time it is the font from which all her power flows" (*SC* 10). So in the celebration of the sacraments and particularly the Eucharist we draw spiritual strength as if from a fresh spring and receive God's grace, which is communicated to us "in spirit and truth" (Jn 4:23).

At Jacob's well, Jesus says to the Samaritan woman and to all of us: "but those who drink of the water that I will give them will never be thirsty. The water that I will give will become in them a spring of water gushing up to eternal life" (Jn 4:14). Christ baptizes us with the water of everlasting life. In the Eucharist he gives himself to us as the living bread: "and the bread that I will give for the life of the world is my flesh" (Jn 6:51).

The cultural criticism of the prophets and Jesus was not directed at the symbolic expression of our worship and glorifi-cation of God that springs from our physical and social nature. Liberal theology appealed in vain to Jesus in order to reduce Christianity to ethics and the bourgeois personality ideal. Even less does Communism have the right to turn Jesus into the first socialist. And it needs to be added here that the gospel grasps man's personality and social nature metaphysically and empir-ically more profoundly than all the epigonic reductions that invoke Jesus, whom they then judge and exploit according to their own norms.

"I desire mercy, not sacrifice," Jesus twice (Mt 9:13, 12:7) quotes the prophet Hosea, where it is written: "For I desire steadfast love and not sacrifice, the knowledge of God rather than burnt-offerings" (Hos 6:6). Indeed it is not the ritual per-formance of Old Testament sacrifices, regardless of the content it is meant to express, and the intention of the faithful that is crucial. "The sacrifice acceptable to God is a broken spirit; a broken and contrite heart" (Ps 51:17). The visible sacrifices in the Old Testament were not to be abolished; rather their inner truth was to be revealed as a celebration of thanksgiving and propitiation (cf. Ps 51:19f.).

The sacrifice that God's Incarnate Son offered up to his Father is a sacrifice in which surrendering one's life is identical with mercy. So the symbol of this sacrifice is not something distinct from him but his own body. Thus on the Cross Jesus supersedes all the sacrifices of previous ages and accomplishes their deepest intention of worshipping God in thanksgiving for everything that we have received from him. He is the sacrificing Priest in his person and in his will to offer up his life. He is the sacrificial victim in his body and the act of oblation in the love with which he vicariously took our sins upon himself and in redeeming us brought us into communion with God.

"Consequently, when Christ came into the world, he said, 'Sacrifices and offerings you have not desired, but a body you have prepared for me' [. . .] then he added, 'See, I have come to do your will.'[. . .] And it is by God's will that we have been sanctified through the offering of the body of Jesus Christ once for all" (Heb 10:5–10). So it is Jesus Christ himself, both sacrificial priest and sacrificial offering in one, who in the Eucharist that the Church celebrates in memory of him leads us through his Cross to our resurrection, for "having been made perfect, he became the source of eternal salvation for all who obey him, having been designated by God a high priest according to the order of Melchizedek" (Heb 5:9f.). When the Church celebrates the sacrifice of God's mercy and of eternal salvation in the divine liturgy (cf. Council of Trent: DH 1529, 1740), she is not performing an empty rite but rather sacramentally re-presenting, that is, making present, Christ's sacrifice. The eucharistic sacrifice does not constitute an alternative to the physical and spiritual works of mercy; rather, it is the source of all *diakonia.*

Thus the Second Vatican Council can state in the Constitution on the Sacred Liturgy:

> Rightly, then, the liturgy is considered as an exercise
> of the priestly office of Jesus Christ. In the liturgy

the sanctification of the man is signified by signs perceptible to the senses, and is effected in a way which corresponds with each of these signs; in the liturgy the whole public worship is performed by the Mystical Body of Jesus Christ, that is, by the Head and his members. From this it follows that every liturgical celebration, because it is an action of Christ the priest and of his Body which is the Church, is a sacred action surpassing all others; no other action of the Church can equal its efficacy by the same title and to the same degree. (*SC* 7)

Immanuel Kant (1724–1804), in his work *Die Religion innerhalb der Grenzen der bloßen Vernunft* (1793: *Religion within the Limits of Bare Reason*), advances the following premise: "Religion is (subjectively considered) the recognition of all our duties as divine commands" (IV,1), thus reducing the worship of God to the fulfillment of moral imperatives. Then follows the conclusion, as "a principle requiring no proof," that sacramental liturgy as adoration and worship of God can only be "mere religious delusion and counterfeit service of God," for apart from a good conduct of life there is nothing that the human being can do "to become well-pleasing to God," (*Religion within the Limits* IV,2, §2). But it is not before a postulate of practical reason that Moses falls to his knees at the sight of the burning bush and takes off his sandals on "holy ground" (Ex 3:5) or that the Messiah spends the night before his Passion and Cross with his Father in prayer on the Mount of Olives. Before the God of a heartless ethics of duty you cannot sing, play, rejoice, and enjoy life.

With this Kant nourished the arrogant sense of superiority of the liberal nineteenth-century bourgeoisie, who derided the "churchgoers," that is, the faithful, practicing Christians, as self-righteous Pharisees for fulfilling their Sunday Mass obligation and as being kept in a state of dependency (*unmündig*) by the clergy for "listening to the Church." People would go to church for a religious concert so as to experience themselves through the medium of music, but not in order to lift up their souls to God and "obtain the freedom of the glory of the children of God" (Rom 8:21). We Christians celebrate the liturgy to the glory of God and for the salvation of man.

"Praise the LORD! Sing to the LORD a new song, his praise in the assembly of the faithful. Let Israel be glad in its Maker; let the children of Zion rejoice in their King. Let them praise his name with dancing, making melody to him with tambourine and lyre. For the LORD takes pleasure in his people; he adorns the humble with victory. Let the faithful exult in glory; let them sing for joy on their couches" (Ps 149:1–5).

But dogma and liturgy are not about making ourselves well-pleasing to God by observing dogmas and rites. On the contrary, it is only in professing and practicing our faith that we become aware of the good will of God that we have already received in his Son.

"But when the goodness and loving-kindness of God our Saviour appeared, he saved us, not because of any works of righteousness that we had done, but according to his mercy, through the water of rebirth and renewal by the Holy Spirit. This Spirit he poured out on us richly through Jesus Christ our Saviour, so that, having been justified by his grace, we might become heirs according to the hope of eternal life" (Ti 3:4–7).

In her liturgy, the Church experiences and professes the presence of Christ, which he has promised us until he comes again at the end of the world to offer up the whole of creation to his Father for the eternal glorification of God.

"To accomplish so great a work, Christ is always present in his Church, especially in her liturgical celebrations" (*SC* 7): in the sacrifice of the Mass, in the person of the priest, under the eucharistic species, in the sacraments, and in the words that are proclaimed.

In the Eucharist the unity of the ministerial priesthood and the priesthood of all the faithful is supremely realized and visible (cf. *LG* 10). In the bishop, Christ the high priest and pastor is present and represented in the midst of his flock (cf. *SC* 41).

For this reason, presiding at the celebration of the Eucharist, where he represents Christ as the head of the Church, constitutes the pinnacle of the priest's mandate and mission. For Christ is present in his minister, "the same now offering, through the ministry of priests, who formerly offered himself on the cross" (*SC* 7; DH 1743).

The authority to offer Christ's sacrifice in the sacrifice of the Mass and the authority to consecrate were not assigned to priests through an act of canon law or the facticity of an old custom; rather, it results from the nature of the Sacrament of Holy Orders, the Eucharist, the sacramental Body of Christ, and the Church, the Mystical Body of Christ.

Although there is no biblical reference for this in the sense of a specific, somewhat ahistorical method of proof, this does not argue against the fact that this authority belongs to the apostles and thus to their successors in the office of bishop and presbyter by virtue of divine law. The biblical writings provide us with a testimony to the Church's sacred history and Creed, but not with a theological treatise. If the Corinthians had not given reason to say a few words on their misconduct at the Eucharist, we would hardly have any proof in Paul's epistles of the existence and central significance of the Lord's Supper.

The apostolic authority and the special commission to celebrate the liturgical memorial of Christ's Passion until he comes again results in the overseers of the Church also presiding at the Sacrament of the Body of Christ (*corpus Christi sacramentale*), from which the Church as his body (*corpus Christi ecclesiale*) lives and is built up.

In the Church's praxis at the time of the New Testament witness as well as in the documents immediately following this there are no "laity," that is, people without any apostolic authority and mission, who might appear as overseers of the churches or presiders at celebrations of the Eucharist. When Paul admonished the Corinthians to celebrate the Lord's Supper in God's Church in the spirit of Jesus' institution of the Eucharist at the Last Supper with his disciples before his Passion, there was no reason to speak of who presided at the celebration (cf. 1 Cor 11:20ff.). There is nowhere any mention of a community as a collection of lay people without apostolic authority.

In the letter from the Roman church to the church in Corinth forty years after the apostle's letter to them, when there were certainly people still living who had known Paul, it was described as a great sin to eject bishops and presbyters "who have blamelessly and holily fulfilled [their] duties" (1 *Clem* 44,44). Two decades later, Ignatius of Antioch makes the equation: wherever Christ is, there is the Catholic Church, and where the bishop is, there the community should be. And without the bishop there is no secure and valid Eucharist and no sacraments (cf. *IgnSmy* 8).

For the unity is realized in the *one* Eucharist on the *one* altar of the sacrifice of Christ's flesh and blood and represented in the *one* bishop along with his presbytery and deacons (cf. *IgnPhil* 4).

Scarcely a century later (ca. AD 150), Justin Martyr testifies to the role of the priest in his First Apology: "There is then brought to the president of the brethren bread and a cup of wine mixed with water; and he taking them, gives praise and glory to the Father of the universe, through the name of the Son and of the Holy Ghost, and offers thanks at considerable length for our being counted worthy to receive these things at his hands. And when he has concluded the prayers and thanksgivings, all the people present express their assent by saying Amen" (1 *Apol.* 65). The prerequisite for participation in the Eucharist is Baptism for the remission of sins and being reborn as a child of God, assent to the Church's doctrine, and willingness to live according to Christ's instructions. For we truly receive, through the transubstantiation of the gifts of bread and wine, "the flesh and blood of that Jesus who was made flesh" (1 *Apol.* 66; cf. *Did.* 14,1).

At the beginning of the third century, according to the first consecration liturgy that has been handed down to us in its entirety, the authority to offer the sacred sacrifice, to consecrate, and to forgive sins was conferred on the bishops and presbyters along with the "spirit of high priesthood" (*TA* 3, 4). This is an expression of a divinely revealed truth. The connection between the sacramental priesthood and the offering of the eucharistic sacrifice is not positivistically or consuetudinally founded, but based rather on the sacramentality of the sacrifice of the Mass and the priesthood.

And for this reason the Council of Trent states over against the Protestants: "Since, therefore, in the New Testament the Catholic Church has received from the institution of Christ the holy, visible sacrifice of the Eucharist, it must also be acknowledged that there exists in the Church a new visible and external priesthood" (DH 1764).

The Paschal Mystery of Christ's Passion, his sacrifice on the altar of the Cross, and his victory over death, sin, and the devil in his Resurrection from the dead are the center of gravity of the whole of salvation history, which also includes the whole cosmos. When Christ's giving of himself to the Father is made present in holy Mass and we are drawn into community with the Father and the Holy Spirit through the sacramental eating of his Body and Blood, then the celebration of the Eucharist is the apex of priestly ministry and the fount from which it draws its spiritual strength (cf. *LG* 11). How could a priest renew and bring to life the grace and spirit of his ministry more profoundly and more richly than in uniting himself daily with Christ's sacrificial self-giving for the salvation of the world in the eucharistic sacrifice and in sacramental communion with Christ?

Union with the crucified and resurrected Lord took place once in an eternally valid way at our Baptism. By participating devoutly and actively in the celebration of the eucharistic sacrifice (*participatio actuosa*), the old sinful, selfish person in us should daily die away so that the new person might arise who lives for God. In every Eucharist, the priests, who represent Christ as the head (cf. *PO* 13), and all the faithful as members of this body experience the truth of being children of God: "So you also must consider yourselves dead to sin and alive to God in Christ Jesus" (Rom 6:11).

God, our Father, is supremely worshipped and adored when the Church, vicariously for mankind and the whole of creation, gives thanks through and in Christ for his communicating himself to us in the Holy Spirit as truth and life. In the Eucharist, the rejoicing of the redeemed is collected and offered to God by the priest in the sacrificial vessel. And the priest experiences the noblest hour of his day when he recognizes in the sacrifice of the Mass that God "has made us competent to be ministers of a new covenant" (2 Cor 3:6). It is "the ministry of the Spirit" that has "come in glory" and will lead not to death, but to life, to justice and to glory (cf. 2 Cor 3:7–11).

The role of the faithful here is not that of mere bystanders and passive recipients of the gifts of salvation. Through the ministry of the priests they join the sacrifices of their lives with the sacrifice of Christ's Church.

The faithful "should give thanks to God; by offering the Immaculate Victim, not only through the hands of the priest, but also with him, they should learn also to offer themselves; through Christ the Mediator, they should be drawn day by day into ever more perfect union with God and with each other, so that finally God may be all in all" (*SC* 48).

MINISTERS FOR GOVERNING

Like the People of God liberated from slavery in Egypt, Christ's Church is guided safely by God on her pilgrimage through the desert and the grassland, the lows and highs, into the Promised Land and the heavenly Jerusalem. The most impressive and appealing expression of God's being there for his people is in the image of him as Israel's shepherd. Just as a shepherd fetches back the scattered sheep, binds up the wounded ones, and takes attentive and loving care of them all, so God looks after all of us. He is not the God of speculative idealism, of the working hypothesis of physico-theology and deism, or the postulate of moral reason; rather, he is the Creator of heaven and earth. He created men and women in his image and likeness (Gen 1:27).

Addressing God and referring to mankind, Psalm 8 states: "You have crowned them with glory and honour. You have given them dominion over the works of your hands" (5f.).

We understand God's salvific work towards us when we open ourselves to his promises: "They shall know that I, the LORD their God, am with them, and that they, the house of Israel, are my people, says the Lord GOD. You are my sheep, the sheep of my pasture, and I am your God, says the Lord GOD" (Ezek 34:30f.).

The messianic promise fulfilled in Jesus is given to us in the figure of David, the shepherd king. He is "a ruler who is to shepherd my people Israel" (Mt 2:6; cf. Micah 5:2–4), the Immanuel, God with us (Mt 1:23). Jesus is the "one shepherd" whom God will set over his people (cf. Ezek 34:23).

Jesus reveals the mystery of his person and his mission from the Father: "I am the good shepherd. The good shepherd lays down his life for the sheep. [. . .] I am the good shepherd. I know my own and my own know me, just as the Father knows me and I know the Father. And I lay down my life for the sheep" (Jn 10:11, 14f.).

Peter together with the apostles (Jn 21:15) and their successors in the office of bishops and priests have been made "overseers, to shepherd the church of God" by the Holy Spirit (Acts 20:28), "to tend the flock of God" in the name of Christ, "the chief shepherd" (1 Pt 5:2–4; cf. Heb 13:20) and "the shepherd and guardian of your souls" (1 Pt 2:25).

The governance of the Church is thus completely Christologically and pneumatologically determined. Bishops and priests would essentially misinterpret their power (*potestas sacra*) if they took the political and organizational exercise of power as the model for their pastoral office.

Willingness to lay down your life for the faithful entrusted to you is what shows how the specific difference between an office of governance in an ecclesial society and one in a political society is to be defined. It is not merely bloody martyrdom that is meant by this; it also means the readiness, day in and day out, to put one's own interests and wishes last. In his daily celebration of the sacrifice of the Mass the priest receives the strength to sacrifice himself for the kingdom of God.

The higher the responsibility he takes on, the greater are the demands made on the priest. The spiritual, intellectual, and moral demands of clerical office belong preeminently and in an exemplary fashion to the bishop since he is the father of his priests and of all the faithful. He teaches, sanctifies, and governs the Church with the love with which Christ gave himself up for his bride, the Church (cf. Eph 5:25f.). Following Jerome, Augustine, John Chrysostom, and the *Regula pastoralis*, where Gregory the Great explains the saying "whoever aspires to the office of bishop desires a noble task" (1 Tim 3:1), Thomas Aquinas says that precisely the bishop with his preparedness to be martyred must distinguish his office from political influence and prestige.

A man is no bishop after Jesus' heart if he loves to precede rather than to profit others "*ut intelligat non se esse episcopum qui praeesse dilexerit, non prodesse*" (Thomas Aquinas, *S.th.* II-II q.185 a.1 ad 1). The *cursus honorum* when assuming public office is not the right level of comparison for the sequence of rising through ecclesial offices from deacon to priest, and to bishop, cardinal, and pope.

Quite rightly, higher honor is due to higher office. But anyone who recognizes the vanity of everything under the sun will rejoice at the greatness of his service to the salvation of his fellow believers, but at the same time shudder at the possibility of failure in his responsibility for the "salvation of souls" (1 Pt 1:9). When praising the fact that someone aspires to the great task of being a bishop, Aquinas adds that the bishop must be above reproach, "as if he wanted to say: I praise what you seek, but learn first what it is you seek—*laudo quod quaeritis, sed discite quid quaeratis*" (Thomas Aquinas, *S.th.* II-II q.185 a.1 ad 1).

In comparing perfection in the religious state and in the office of bishop, it has to be said that the bishop must be perfect in order to lead others to perfection and sanctification. No one gives himself the honor of higher ecclesial office; a person is

honored with it by God "only when called by God" (Heb 5:4).
But then his love of God and care for the salvation of others
do not permit him to evade God's call either. Unlike in the religious state, the perfection of priests and bishops does not lie in
voluntarily following the evangelical counsels but rather in the
shepherd's love, which does not relate to his own perfection but
rather to that of others. Here perfection is to be understood in
the biblical sense of directing one's life towards God as its goal
and is not limited to merely leading a morally irreproachable life.
Jesus asks Peter, whom he wants to make the universal shepherd
of his Church: "[D]o you love *me* more than these?" (Jn 21:15,
italics mine).

Thus Jesus also indicates the criterion for selecting suitable
candidates for the office of bishop, namely, "his pre-eminence
in the love of God—*eminentia divinae dilectionis*" (Thomas Aquinas, *S.th.* II-II q.185, a.3 ad 1). The highest ecclesial authority,
which appoints or affirms bishops, must not make love for a
friend or the latter's vain and narcissistic striving for a position of
honor its criterion, which must instead be solely his greater love
for God and willingness to give his life for the sheep of God's
flock. Anyone who appoints a bishop or priest to office for his
own benefit or to satisfy the appointee's vanity "sins mortally"
(Thomas Aquinas, *S.th.* II-II q.185 a.3). Rather, he must appoint
the person who loves Jesus more than himself and is therefore
the "one who is best for governing the Church, one namely who
is able to instruct, defend, and govern the Church peacefully"
(Thomas Aquinas, *S.th.* II-II q.185 a.3).

When we speak of a priest after the heart of the crucified
Jesus, from whose pierced side "blood and water came out" (Jn
19:34), we are not clicking on some sentimental image from the
piety of a past epoch. Being able to feel your heart beating for
others in your own breast in their search for truth and love—that
is what distinguishes the shepherd from the hired hand. "The
good shepherd lays down his life for the sheep. The hired hand,
who is not the shepherd and does not own the sheep, sees the
wolf coming and leaves the sheep and runs away" (Jn 10:11f.).

It is not his brilliant gifts, the panache of his homiletic rhetoric, and his skill in every pastoral technique that fire the souls of his flock but rather the love of the good shepherd, no matter how inexpert he may be at religious education.

When examining our consciences, let us measure all we say and do in proclamation and pastoral care according to the highest norms: "If I speak in the tongues of mortals and of angels [. . . and] if I have prophetic powers, and understand all mysteries and all knowledge, and if I have all faith, so as to remove mountains, but do not have love, I am nothing" (1 Cor 13:1f.).

The love of the good shepherd preserves us from restless activism when we are snowed under with work and worries and from inner emigration when we feel there is no point in anything anymore.

But *we* did not redeem the world, nor can we do so in the future. On the other hand, we must not bury the talents we have received from the Lord. What distinguishes us priests is an apostolic zeal as if everything depended on us and a comforted equanimity in the knowledge that Jesus Christ has already done all that is necessary for the salvation of the world. Everyone should, with the grace God has given them, work on building the house of God; but no one can "lay any foundation other than the one that has been laid; that foundation is Jesus Christ" (1 Cor 3:11).

It will be revealed in the end whether we have done our duty when "the fire will test what sort of work each has done" and "the builder will receive a reward" (1 Cor 3:13f.).

The field of work in individual pastoral care, the parish, the diocese, and the universal Church is immense and never-ending. Despite the chronic lack of an adequate number of priests, the aim of a diocesan or nationwide "pastoral plan" must be to keep the parishes at a manageable size or to achieve this. The local church, and within it the parish, should reflect the essence of the Church as God's family and enable people to experience it as such. On account of this family quality of the local church, we should set as our norm having one priest for every thousand faithful. Linked to this is also the priest's lifestyle and way of working in this family. The celibate life is not to be confused with the lifestyle of singles in a city. A *vita communis*—in whatever concrete form this may take—follows from the *communio* nature of apostolic ministry. Collaboration with religious and with licensed lay people is also perfectly in keeping with the nature of priestly ministry. After all, the priest has become a spiritual father in Christ for the faithful, following the example of the apostle (cf. 1 Cor 4:15f.). In his parish family, he should "not speak harshly to an older man, but speak to him as to a father, to younger men as brothers, to older women as mothers, to younger women as sisters—with absolute purity" (1 Tim 5:1f.).

In the course of my times of hands-on work as a curate and helping out in parishes while I was a university professor and during my ten years as diocesan bishop, I have gone through the cycle of the Christian preaching and pastoral year forty times to date.

The liturgical year forms the *cantus firmus* of evangelization. The events of salvation history and the commemoration of the saints shape our attitude towards our faith and the world we live in. With the high degree of specialization in a society based on the division of labor, it is the Catholic priest who has dealings with every generation each week. Visits to the kindergarten, youth activities, and senior citizens' afternoons bring the priest into contact with people of all ages in all their joys and sorrows. With liturgies for special occasions and in administering the sacraments he encounters people at the turning points in their lives. He promotes responsibility for the world among the laity in Church clubs, associations, and charitable organizations. The priest does not close his heart to anyone who is seeking, has doubts, or is in need. And he also shows patience towards those who oppose him and make his life difficult. And as Christ's coworkers we endeavor to make sure that "We are putting no obstacle in anyone's way, so that no fault may be found with our ministry, but as servants of God we have commended ourselves in every way: through great endurance, in afflictions, hardships, calamities, [. . .]; by purity, knowledge, patience, kindness, holiness of spirit, genuine love, truthful speech, and the power of God; with the weapons of righteousness for the right hand and for the left; in honour and dishonour, in ill repute and good repute" (2 Cor 6:3–8).

In the Decree on the Ministry and Life of Priests the Second Vatican Council unfolds the wide-ranging ministry of priests in Christ's pastoral service and concludes with a warning and a definitive clarification of the nature of priestly ministry: "In building the Christian community, priests are never to put themselves at the service of some human faction of ideology, but, as heralds of the Gospel and shepherds of the Church, they are to spend themselves for the spiritual growth of the Body of Christ" (*PO* 6).

11.

CLERICAL LIFE IN PRAYER AND SACRIFICE

Dear Confreres and Fellow Christians,

Bishops, priests, and deacons are rightly called "clerics." Luther objected to this, arguing that because of the universal priesthood, all Christians, not just ordained priests, belonged to the clerical state. But the "laity" do not stand outside the sanctuary in the Catholic understanding since they—like the pastors of the Church—are baptized in the name of the Father and the Son and the Holy Spirit and sealed with the Holy Spirit in Confirmation. And so they, too, lead a spiritual[15] life in personal and common prayer. They are members of the Body of Christ and say to God through Christ: Abba, Father.

It was merely an effective publicity ploy to argue that the mediating ministry of ordained priests was a negation of the laity's direct access to God. Priests are, after all, not mediators to a distant God who is inaccessible to the masses. They themselves do not have exclusive access to an absolutely remote transcendence like some privileged caste. Nor do they "own" the means of grace so as to be able to administer them as they see fit and according to their own financial and political interests without seriously abusing them.

Instead, what the apostles and their successors "as servants of Christ and stewards of God's mysteries" (1 Cor 4:1) communicate in preaching the gospel and celebrating Christ's sacraments is the reconciliation of mankind with God, a reconciliation that has already happened, having been brought about once and for all by Christ on the Cross. Therefore priests serve the building up of the Church in the Holy Spirit. They promote the intensive and extensive growth of the Church in Christ and towards Christ, the head of the Church.

Freed from the false categories that led to the classic misunderstanding in the Reformation period, Vatican II expresses the valid Catholic teaching: "The ministerial priest (*sacerdos ministerialis*), by the sacred power (*potestate sacra*) he enjoys, teaches and rules the priestly people; acting in the person of Christ, he makes present the Eucharistic sacrifice, and offers it to God in the name of all the people. But the faithful, in virtue of their royal priesthood, join in the offering of the Eucharist. They likewise exercise that priesthood in receiving the sacraments, in prayer and thanksgiving, in the witness of a holy life, and by self-denial and active charity" (*LG* 10).

So the Catholic priest does not stand between God and the "laity," separating the two. Rather, the Church's unity with Christ her head is reflected figuratively and symbolically in the sacramental celebration of the whole Church. Christ acts as her head through the liturgical words and signs of the priest. And he mediates his salvation to the members of his Body, through whom he acts on the world. Hence it is through the ministry of the whole Church, especially in the apostolate of the laity, too, that people are to be won for Christ so that the world might be permeated with the Spirit of Christ.

As Catholics, there is nothing to prevent us from subscribing to Luther's proposition that all the baptized belong to the clerical state without accepting his jibe at the hierarchical priesthood. If the priest is the *typos* of the flock and *imago Christi*, then the demand for a life led in the Spirit of Christ does not apply exclusively to him but rather in the sense that he is to set an example. A priest should lead a spiritual life. This refers to the piety that daily renews in him afresh the spirit of his apostolic zeal. He is for the flock entrusted to him a model for the discipleship of Christ and keeping Christ's commandments. As a preacher of the faith, he must also be particularly competent in the true teaching of the Church and the intellectual defense of the faith (cf. 1 Pt 3:15). A priest today must be an educated man with good manners and respectful behavior.

Only if we live in deep communion with Christ, whose messengers and witnesses we are as priests, can we say to the faithful with both humility and certainty: "Be imitators of me, as I am of Christ" (1 Cor 11:1). For presbyters are "examples (*typoi*) to the flock" (1 Pt 5:3). And for the faithful it holds true: "Remember your leaders, those who spoke the word of God to you; consider the outcome of their way of life, and imitate their faith" (Heb 13:7).

The spirituality of bishops and priests is linked to their official mission. Because they govern, sanctify, and instruct the community in the person of Christ, they should allow themselves to be completely conformed to the image of Christ in their inner lives:

> In the first place, the shepherds of Christ's flock must holily and eagerly, humbly and courageously carry out their ministry, in imitation of the eternal high Priest, the Shepherd and Guardian of our souls. They ought to fulfill this duty in such a way that it will be the principal means also of their own sanctification. Those chosen for the fullness of the priesthood are granted the ability of exercising the perfect duty of pastoral charity by the grace of the Sacrament of Orders. This perfect duty of pastoral charity (cf. 1 Pt 5:3) is exercised in every form of episcopal care and service, prayer, sacrifice and preaching. By this same sacramental grace, they are given the courage necessary to lay down their lives for their sheep, and the ability of promoting greater holiness in the Church by their daily example, having become a pattern for their flock. (*LG* 41)

St. John Chrysostom derives the demand for priests to live a holy and exemplary life from the supreme dignity of their office.

For he who acts as an ambassador on behalf of the
whole city, indeed of the whole world, and prays that
God would be merciful to the sins of all, not only of
the living, but also of the departed, what manner of
man ought he to be? [. . .] And whenever he invokes
the Holy Spirit, and offers the most dread sacrifice,
and constantly handles the common Lord of all, tell
me what rank shall we give him? What great purity
and what real piety must we demand of him? For
consider what manner of hands they ought to be
which minister in these things, and of what kind his
tongue which utters such words, and ought not the
soul which receives so great a spirit to be purer and
holier than anything in the world? (*De sac.* VI,4)

The priest's spirituality 1) feeds on a deep connection with
God; 2) shows itself in the radical nature of his discipleship of
Christ; 3) supports the spiritual life of the servants of God.

THE FIRST PRAY-ER
IN THE COMMUNITY

In my time at the seminary in Mainz, my revered bishop, Her-
mann Cardinal Volk (1903–1988), gave us spiritual addresses
about our intended vocation. Among the many valuable tips
he gave us, one impressive formulation has stuck particularly
in my memory: the priest is the first pray-er in the community.

The Church is indeed a community of the faith that we have
received. But for this very reason she is also a community of
prayer. God speaks to us in his revelation, and we address him
in prayer as "Abba, Father."

In the prayer that Jesus gave to his Church it is not the
individual speaking privately to God; rather, we address God
publicly and together: "Our Father, who art in heaven." The
Paternoster illustrates the form and content of Christian prayer.
We do not pray to some metaphysical abstraction, to deified

earthly powers, or to the products of a mythological imagination. God is trinitarian: we speak personally to the Father through the Son in the Holy Spirit, who is poured out into our hearts. We are sons and daughters of God, and so it is a prayer prayed in the spirit of a child's love, not in a spirit of calculation and a fear of offending against some unknown taboo and thus incurring the "wrath of the gods." Since we are created in God's image and likeness and he has given us the earth as our common home, right from the start there has been no dialectical relationship of opposition and competition between God and man. God loses nothing and gains nothing in creating mankind. He has given us our existence and leads us in his gracious providence to the goal of our lives: the vision of God face to face. God created us in his Word so as to reveal his loving-kindness and to realize our supernatural calling by being taken up into his trinitarian life in all eternity. Christian prayer consists in glorifying God and requesting the gifts that we need for our natural and supernatural lives.

When he prays, the priest does not stand alone before God while the congregation waits at a great distance from him until he returns like Moses from the mountain or like the high priest of the old covenant coming back out of the holy of holies in the Temple and appearing before the people in the vestibule. The priest visibly represents the person of Christ as the head of the Body; but the head never functions effectively without its body and limbs, its members. A community of action exists between priest and congregation in the hearing of the word, in worshipping God, in asking his mercy, and in intercessory prayers for the world.

In this sense he is as the leader of the congregation also its leader in prayer. At the same time it is clear that every sacrament and sacramental, as well as every other form of the Church's individual and collective prayer, is oriented towards the Eucharist, in which they are all gathered together as their culmination.

The priest prays in the name of Christ vicariously for the Church, not for his personal sanctification or even just for the strength to fulfill his mission well. In addition to the individual prayers of the kind every Christian says, there are official intercessions that lend greater efficacy to his ministry of sanctification. Unlike the subjective efficacy of the sacraments (*ex opere operato*), the prayers of the priest have the subjective efficacy of a blessing (*ex opere operantis*) for the faithful entrusted to him. Paul, who has received through Christ "grace and apostleship to bring about the obedience of faith among all the Gentiles for the sake of his name," writes to "all God's beloved in Rome, who are called to be saints" (Rom 1:5–7): "First, I thank my God through Jesus Christ for all of you, because your faith is proclaimed throughout the world. For God, whom I serve with my spirit by announcing the gospel of his Son, is my witness that without ceasing I remember you always in my prayers" (Rom 1:8f.). It is a prayer in keeping with the apostolate to bring about the growth of salvific grace as salvation for all. We are not just concerned with personal and private matters.

When a candidate stands before the altar to be ordained as a servant of the Church, the bishop asks him whether he professes the faith of the Church and if he is willing to say the prayers of the Church, the Divine Office, on behalf of the faithful.

Jesus himself, the high priest of the new covenant and "the great shepherd of the sheep" (Heb 13:20), prayed on the Mount of Olives in the night before his vicarious and salvific Passion "with loud cries and tears, to the one who was able to save him from death, and he was heard" (Heb 5:7). And Jesus often withdrew into solitude with his disciples in order to pray to the Father, whose mission for the salvation of the world he had obediently taken upon himself (e.g., Lk 9:18).

The intercessory prayer of the priest in solitude or in a "celebrating community" is far from being a spiritual pleasure, a switching-off and being alone. Jesus' prayers, his mission from the Father for the salvation of the world right down to the tears and fears on the Mount of Olives—these all serve as a model for the prayers of the pastors who commend the sheep of his flock through Jesus to the heavenly Father.

In his prayer life, the priest should set a good example for the faithful. The apostle's exhortation applies first and foremost to the overseers of the Church, but along with them to the whole community: "Pray in the Spirit at all times in every prayer and supplication. To that end keep alert and always persevere in supplication for all the saints. Pray also for me, so that when I speak, a message may be given to me to make known with boldness the mystery of the gospel, for which I am an ambassador in chains" (Eph 6:18–20). Christian prayer differs from heaping up "empty phrases as the Gentiles do" (Mt 6:7), what we would nowadays call the mechanical reciting of formulaic prayers. The words of prayer are the prayer's body, and the love of God and neighbor its soul.

Let us at our altar through the High Priest Jesus, who suffered "in order to sanctify the people by his own blood" (Heb 13:12), "continually offer a sacrifice of praise to God, that is, the fruit of lips that confess his name. Do not neglect to do good and to share what you have, for such sacrifices are pleasing to God" (Heb 13:15f.).

Contained in the Church's Divine Office and distributed across the canonical hours (Matins, Lauds, Vespers, Compline) throughout the liturgical year, all 150 psalms are to be found along with many biblical and patristic readings; these provide the priest with spiritual nourishment and orientation in his relationship to the living God in every conceivable situation of human life with all its light and shade, its highs and lows. Nothing human is unknown to God or can remain hidden from him. Since God adopted us completely and unconditionally in Christ, the God-Man, we can also apply the patristic Christological principle of "all that he assumed he also saved" to priestly prayer. Time devoted to prayer is not at the expense of pastoral care; rather, it preserves the priest from the routine of a Church functionary. Anyone who learns in prayer to love God ever more deeply will be a witness in pastoral care to God's love, which opens the human heart for the infusion of the heavenly virtues of the faith: the hope and love through which we are justified and sanctified. Referring to the Divine Office, Vatican II states: "Therefore, when this wonderful song of praise is rightly performed by priests and others [. . .], then it is truly the voice of the bride addressed to her bridegroom; it is the very prayer which Christ himself, together with his body, addresses to the Father. Hence all who render this service are not only fulfilling a duty of the Church, but also are sharing in the greatest honor of Christ's spouse, for by offering these praises to God they are standing before God's throne in the name of the Church their Mother" (*SC* 84f.).

In difficult times, when all our toil and suffering seem in vain, we should remember that we are not the true shepherd of God's flock but merely shepherds in his name, and that we ourselves, like the lost sheep, also need to be led by him.

"The Lord is my shepherd, I shall not want. [. . .] Even though I walk through the darkest valley, I fear no evil; for you are with me; your rod and your staff—they comfort me" (Ps 23:1, 4).

Let us look at the goal of our ministry as shepherds of the Church in Christ's name: "And when the chief shepherd appears, you will win the crown of glory that never fades away" (1 Pt 5:4).

Disciples of Jesus, Who Gave His Life *Pro Nobis*

All Christians are called to follow Christ. This discipleship is not confined to just reorienting how we live our lives according to a role model or a moral ideal. Discipleship of Christ, the Son of God and preacher of God's kingdom, has a sacramental dimension. In Baptism we are conformed to the crucified and risen Christ. As children of God, we are raised up to the supreme goal of our calling: gracious fellowship with God the Father, the Son, and the Holy Spirit in the love that is God himself.

Through being signed with a special character in sacred ordination, priests "are conformed to Christ the Priest in such a way that they can act in the person of Christ the Head" (*PO* 2). This *configuratio Christo Sacerdoti* constitutes the priests' specific form of following Christ in their apostolic ministry. From among the wide circle of his disciples, Jesus chose the small group of the Twelve so that they would be *with him* (*cum illo*). And their community of life with Jesus, who lives with the Father in the Holy Spirit, is the basis of their mission as his messengers, in whom he himself comes to mankind.

They align themselves to Christ's way of thinking. They do not "lord it over" those in their charge (1 Pt 5:3) and do not imitate secular potentates. It is not about financial gain and vain careerism. The nature of their mission is to serve the salvation of mankind. And so what applies to them first and foremost is: "Let the same mind be in you that was in Christ Jesus" (Phil 2:5). This means imitating Christ's obedience to the Father, to whose will he subordinates himself in fulfilling his mission right up to his Passion and death on the Cross, and the poverty of the Son of Man, who does not own even a stone on which to lay his head, and forgoing possessions and family—all these are signs of a special calling to follow Christ unconditionally.

The three evangelical counsels of poverty for Christ's sake, chastity in a celibate life, and the formation of the will in accordance with Jesus' obedience towards his Father are all gospel based. Since wealth, free self-determination, and even marriage are not merely good in themselves but also a means to good, an individual can forgo them for the sake of another means. There can be no exceptions from observing the commandments of moral law and the acknowledgment of the sacraments as means of grace. The evangelical counsels pertain to individual people, not to natural communities such as marriage, the family, and the state. Even for the Church as a whole it would not be an ideal to strive for that everyone should live according to the evangelical counsels. Natural and sacramental marriage is not a concession; it is rather the mainstay of society and the Church.

How the evangelical counsels shaped Eastern and Western monasticism into a state of its own alongside the hierarchy and the "laity" does not belong to our topic here. Luther's view that monasticism in the Catholic Church had been understood as a way of justifying the sinner and was therefore rooted in works piety is contradicted by the whole witness of the magisterium and theology. You don't become a Christian (or even a better first-class Christian) through the evangelical counsels but rather through the granting of grace in the sacraments and "the exercise of the virtues" (*LG* 11) according to God's commandments. Every Christian is called to perfection in being conformed to the crucified and risen Lord. All must observe the commandments, and it is only those who are specially called to it who take on the evangelical counsels as a free act of choice.

The religious state differs from the Christian life of the "laity" in the world only in that it is "easier" to achieve perfection in this form of Christian discipleship (Thomas Aquinas, *S.th.* II-II q.184 a.3). Even though it is easier for the mind of someone called to the evangelical counsels to apply itself to God, being withdrawn from the needs of providing for life, this does not mean that this detachment is "so necessary to man for justice that its absence makes justice impossible; indeed, virtue and justice are not removed if man uses bodily and earthly things in accord with the order of reason" (Thomas Aquinas, *S.c.G.* III, 130).

Of course, the prerequisite for this way of perfection, being most intimately conjoined to God in love, is to be called to this form of life. This neither excludes nor downgrades the other callings and charisms; rather, it builds up the Body of Christ in conjunction with them. They are different ways to the same goal; but love is the true measure of man's perfection and completion in God.

Against the Protestant rejection of a life according to the evangelical counsels and the sole validity of marriage, the Council of Trent reaffirmed the whole of biblical and patristic tradition. However, Canon 10 of the Decree on Marriage (1563) does not emphasize the opposite extreme but rather stresses the relationship between the two legitimate states of Christian life: "If anyone says that the married state surpasses that of virginity or celibacy and that it is not better and happier to remain in virginity or celibacy than to be united in matrimony, let him be anathema" (DH 1810). The comparative refers to the way, not to the goal, and depends on both the individual calling and its being freely accepted (cf. 1 Cor 7:37f.).

The evangelical counsels are not a prerequisite for serving as pastors of the Church; nor, though, do they prevent anyone from taking on the office of priest or bishop. Of course, the ordained priesthood is constitutive for the mission of the Church. When a religious is a priest and above all a bishop, the affairs of his office take precedence over his personal charism and lifestyle. A bishop cannot give the Church's fortune to the poor as if it were his own private property because it is intended for other purposes of the Church's mission, too.

PRIESTLY CELIBACY

Priestly celibacy is not the result of applying one of the three evangelical counsels to the bishop and presbyter. Rather, it has to do with a specific affinity of the pastoral office with the way Christ lived his life and gave it up for his sheep. Christ is the bridegroom of the Church, his bride, to whom he espouses himself in an indissoluble bond through his love and devotion (cf. Eph 5:23–31f.).

Of whom could it be claimed more than of Jesus that he remained celibate "for the sake of the kingdom of heaven" (Mt 19:12)? And what holds true for him also applies to those who exercise his priesthood in the Church: "Very truly, I tell you, unless a grain of wheat falls into the earth and dies, it remains just a single grain; but if it dies, it bears much fruit. Those who love their life lose it, and those who hate their life in this world will keep it for eternal life. Whoever serves me must follow me, and where I am, there will my servant be also. Whoever serves me, the Father will honour" (Jn 12:24–26). If a young man could imagine one day working and living as a priest, then he has to take the decision of his own free will to be prepared to follow Christ right up to the ultimate selflessness that is expressed in the words: "No one has greater love than this, to lay down one's life for one's friends" (Jn 15:13).

That is more than being able to get used to the procedures and demands of a secular job. Many people can imagine themselves running the pastoral activities of a parish, but few are willing to give up living a comfortable middle-class life outside their fixed working hours.

Unlike the three evangelical counsels in which a Christian conforms to a personally given charism and takes a vow, a candidate for the priesthood, trusting in God's help, makes the simple decision to take on this way of life for the sake of exercising priestly ministry.

It therefore cannot be said that someone is persuaded or forced to promise celibacy who does not possess the charism of this evangelical counsel. For "there are eunuchs who have made themselves eunuchs for the sake of the kingdom of heaven" (Mt 19:12). Anyone who is willing and able to adopt this way of life does so as a result of his own free decision. "Let anyone accept this who can" (Mt 19:12). If a priest resigns or is removed from office, he may possibly be granted a dispensation from his voluntary obligation. However, unlike with men and women religious, he cannot be said to have broken a vow. At his ordination to the diaconate he does not (under the currently valid legislation in the Latin Church) take a vow of celibacy but simply promises the bishop to live a celibate life, naturally with the moral and spiritual consequences that result from this.

Even though there have been and still are married priests in the Catholic Church who serve her faithfully, the Church nevertheless (in the Latin Rite) holds fast to celibacy as a norm because it "is held by the Church to be of great value in a special manner for the priestly life" (*PO* 16). So it was not simply for pragmatic reasons that celibacy developed for the priesthood in the first few centuries. Nor is it a positivistically mandated combining of the priesthood with this gospel-based way of life.

Since celibacy "is not demanded by the very nature of the priesthood" (*PO* 16) but rather suggests itself as a result of its inner affinity to the office that visibly represents Christ, the Church's bridegroom, Peter's famous mother-in-law (cf. Mt 8:14) cannot be advanced as an argument against priestly celibacy any more than can the wives who accompanied the apostles (cf. 1 Cor 9:5). When the list of qualifications for a bishop as overseer of the Church also contains the demand that he must be married only once in his life (cf. 1 Tim 3:2), this does not speak against but rather for the affinity of priesthood and celibacy. For a second marriage after a wife's death is ruled out inasmuch as Christ is married once and for all to the Church as his bride. This practice is still today valid for priests in the Catholic and Orthodox Eastern Churches, too. Both East and West share the practice that bishops cannot be married because they eminently represent Christ as the bridegroom of the Church (cf. 2 Cor 11:2).

In the West, the tradition has emerged that also second-degree priests, that is, presbyters, promise celibacy before ordination. The initial celibacy requiring sexual continence of married priests was later turned by canonical legislation into a celibacy of remaining unmarried.[16] The Church's legislation on celibacy in the Latin Rite is justified as a whole and capable of sustaining an individual's life decision only because it is based on an inner analogy between priesthood and the freely chosen renunciation of marriage and family "for the sake of the kingdom of heaven" (Mt 19:12; cf. 1 Cor 7:32ff.).

Vatican II explains it to us as follows:

> Through virginity, then, or celibacy observed for the Kingdom of Heaven, priests are consecrated to Christ by a new and exceptional reason. They adhere to him more easily with an undivided heart, they dedicate themselves more freely in him and through him to the service of God and men, and they more

expeditiously minister to his Kingdom and the work of heavenly regeneration, and thus they are apt to accept, in a broad sense, paternity in Christ. In this way they profess themselves before men as willing to be dedicated to the office committed to them— namely, to commit themselves faithfully to *one* man and to show themselves as a chaste virgin for Christ (cf. 2 Cor 11:2) and thus to evoke the mysterious marriage established by Christ, and fully to be manifested in the future, in which the Church has Christ as her only Spouse (cf. Rev 19:7). They give, moreover, a living sign of the world to come, by a faith and charity already made present, in which the children of the resurrection neither marry nor take wives (cf. Lk 20:35f.). (*PO* 16)

The evangelical counsels and priestly celibacy cannot be derived, and thus devalued, either historically or systematically from the Manichaean contempt for the body or from the prohibition of marriage in some Christian sects. The philosophical and non-Christian religious motivation for freeing oneself from the baser instincts of sex and eros has nothing to do with the Christologically and eschatologically founded celibate way of life of the Catholic priest because a completely different image of man underlies the latter.

Despite all the uncertainties and ambiguities in Christian asceticism and mysticism, it is not a matter of being a little more or less antagonistic to or positive about the pleasures of the body. It is about finding the right approach altogether. Neither a materialistic idolization of the body nor an idealistic spiritualization of man is compatible with theological anthropology. And it has always been a heresy to declare man's corporeal nature to be a source and cause of sin as this goes against the article of faith that God is "the creator of all things, visible and invisible, spiritual and corporeal," as the Fourth Lateran Council (1215) states against the Albigensians and Cathars (DH 800).

Philosophical and theological reflection on the belief that man was created out of soil through God's breathing life-giving breath into him led to the concept of the substantial unity of soul and body. It was not two complete things that were externally joined together or grew together. Everything creaturely is a composite of actual and potential being. Man is constituted in his being through being-there (*Da-sein*) and being-so (*So-sein*), soul and body, personality and sociality. Man is one as a person (*omne ens est unum*): completely with himself (*ganz bei sich*) in his self-reflection, transcendence of the world, and relatedness to the world; nevertheless at the same time involved in the material world in his corporeality and communicating with it (in eating, procreation, linguistic and cultural community). As "spirit in the world" coming from God and "world in the Spirit" going towards God, man is the why of creation (cf. *GS* 14). What follows from this as a metaphysical insight and ethical imperative is man's fundamental self-affirmation and acceptance of himself as a creature of God and thus as a social and historical being made up of body and soul. All creation is an expression of God's goodness and is therefore given the predicate "very good" (Gen 1:31). This applies to the physical form of humankind, created as male and female, especially in the complementarity of the sexes. The reason for sin in the sphere of sex, too, is not to be sought in man's corporeality, let alone in his finitude, which is identical with being created, but rather in his turning away of his own free will from the sacred and sanctifying will of God.

Evil has no nature; otherwise it would have been produced by a necessarily evil "god." Even in the state of the "sin of Adam" human nature is in itself good and both inclined towards good actions and orientated above all to the worship and love of God. In order to reach these goals, man of course needs the grace of forgiveness and to be raised up to being a child of God. Hence, from the Christian point of view, even pagans can enter into a legitimate marriage and in their love and care for their spouse and children contribute to the glorification of God in his creation. However, as a result of original or ancestral sin the natural intellectual, spiritual, and physical givens underwent a certain amount of disintegration. Yet even man's sex drive did not become bad in itself; it can only serve evil when man's free will surrenders to selfishness. Christian sexual ethics by no means requires a man's sexual and erotic desire for a woman or a woman's for a man to be fought against and suppressed; rather, these need to be guided by grace so as to be integrated into personal love in the form of agape.

The modern body-soul (or mind-body) dualism divided up the world into *res cogitans* (thinking thing) and *res extensa* (the extended thing, the thing that exists) (Descartes). Soul and body are now only accidentally linked. Applied to morals, this means either that the spiritual/intellectual part of a person must control the dull promptings of nature as a master does a recalcitrant servant or that the individual should allow his natural urge free rein and merely channel it "sensibly." All that is then left as a criterion is that of the utilitarian ethic of doing no harm to oneself or others. Accordingly, people should gratify their sexual desires and erotic dreams and live them out. They should not allow themselves to be constrained or frustrated by norms that are out of touch with the world and inimical to pleasure and which after all merely lead to double standards. Suppressed sensuality and sexuality then find themselves an outlet in all kinds of perversions—so runs the assumption in the popular and often demagogic sex-education literature with its prejudice against convents, monasteries, and priestly celibacy.

Christian sexual ethics, by contrast, assumes the created goodness of the human body and the inner interpenetration and unity of soul and body. What is crucial here is to categorize as positive both the intellectual capacities of reason and the free will and the psychological emotions and bodily organs.

Every Christian, whether preparing for sacramental marriage or celibacy for the sake of God's kingdom, must be disposed towards the freely chosen way of life through a right understanding of sexuality and eros integrated with one another in agape.

What is vital here is that the visible world is not seen simply as the place where supramundane salvation takes place; instead, the body must be understood as an object of redemption and a means of salvation. "The body is meant not for fornication but for the Lord, and the Lord for the body. [. . .] Or do you not know that your body is a temple of the Holy Spirit within you, which you have from God, and that you are not your own? For you were bought with a price; therefore glorify God in your body" (1 Cor 6:13–19f.).

Creation, Incarnation, the sacramental mediation of salvation, the visible Church—these are all unassailable facts that in every respect rule out an idealizing interpretation of Christianity as "Platonism for the 'people'"[17] as well as its secularization, that is, being transformed into a humanistic program.

We counter these two extremes, both of which can be turned into missiles to launch against the Catholic Church, with the Catholic principle of the *et-et* of the sacramentality of Christian marriage and the voluntary celibacy of many priests and religious undertaken in order to serve the kingdom of God.

12.

THE PRIEST: A THEOLOGICAL EXISTENCE

Dear Confreres, Dear Friends,

The priest of Jesus Christ, the Logos, is a servant of the word, teacher of the faith, and a wise steward of God's house. The capable priest is a Catholic intellectual. St. John Vianney cannot be cited as a counterexample. He was an intellectual and spiritual man, but in his own way. He won't do as a patron saint for messy thinkers and the mentally lazy. "Therefore every scribe who has been trained for the kingdom of heaven is like the master of a household who brings out of his treasure what is new and what is old" (Mt 13:52). But let us not forget that the apostles and their successors are those of whom Jesus said: "Therefore I send you prophets, sages, and scribes, some of whom you will kill and crucify, and some you will flog in your synagogues and pursue from town to town" (Mt 23:34).

A priest does not just have to know the faith as it is summarized in the *Catechism of the Catholic Church*. He must also engage in theology academically and be capable of forming a *well-founded opinion* on questions of faith and morals. Of course, not everyone has the aptitude and calling to put his life at the service of academic theology. Nor is this necessary either for the Church with her great variety of charisms or for the universities with their many different faculties. But in a world that is shaped by science, technology, and global communications, a cleric needs to be for his flock a spiritual man and well-versed in the humanities. A diligent priest will also endeavor to keep both his knowledge and his problem horizon up to date.

Theological studies are not an end in themselves. Theology is in the service of faith and Church. But all of us are in need of mystagogics and catechesis and therefore also of their human mediators, namely the priests of the Church and the teachers of the faith. When it is nourished by a deep spirituality and when it serves the Church in her mediation of supernatural salvation and the divine calling of all mankind, theology does not remain some inward-looking intellectual game. Anyone who recognizes the intrinsic unity of faith and life, which is reflected in the unity of the systematic and practical disciplines of theology, will be equally immune from pursuing a theoretical theology with no heart as from falling prey to a mindless frenzy of activity in pastoral care, a sort of over-the-counter theology.

The seemingly humble, but in reality arrogant, anti-intellectual feeling that regards the writing and studying of academic books as superfluous harms the Church in her intellectual analysis of contemporary issues. The same goes for the vanity of scholars who do not use their talents in the service of truth but rather put them narcissistically on display.

Let us disregard these weaknesses and think instead in the categories of the various charisms that we have been given: "To each is given the manifestation of the Spirit for the common good" (1 Cor 12:7). Let us view the vocation of the Catholic theologian positively and obey the apostle Paul's imperative: "if it is a gift of practical service, let us devote ourselves to serving; if it is teaching, to teaching" (Rom 12:7).

But there is always the justified question of whether there aren't already enough books in the world. Wouldn't we be using our time and energy better if we got practically involved in seeking solutions for the urgent challenges of our time? Hasn't the time come for praxis, and isn't the age of great ideas a thing of the past? Besides, Jesus and the apostles didn't see their mission as being to write books. And every individual receives the faith necessary for his or her salvation from hearing the word and will find salvation by following the way of Jesus Christ to the end in love. There is not a single theological work that you absolutely have to read in order to achieve salvation. But the teachers of the faith, whose sacred duty it is to study theology, must not excuse themselves from it unless they want to sin against the salvation of the flock entrusted to them. Priests, and even more so bishops, have to be familiar with the whole of the Church's teaching and capable of arguing their case to anyone who wishes to know the reasons for faith or who attacks it (cf. Thomas Aquinas, *S.th.* Suppl. q.36 a.2).

Jesus did not write any books. Nevertheless he was able to read from the sacred scriptures and was already capable at the age of twelve of sitting among the teachers in the Temple and, to their astonishment, listening with comprehension and asking questions. "And all who heard him were amazed at his understanding and his answers" (Lk 2:47). He is, after all, the Logos who was with God and is God. In him and through him all things came into being, including everything created and revealed through which we know God. The fullness of all wisdom and life is known in the Word that became flesh (cf. Jn 1–4, 14).

As a human being, Jesus unfolded his many individual teachings and "words of eternal life" (Jn 6:68) in the vocabulary, syntax, and grammar of human language, using the articulation of the finite spirit with all his many ideas and concepts being expressed in the succession of space and time. Yet all of these are both encapsulated in the one un-created Word that he is in his divine nature and proceed from it (cf. Jn 1:1). The one divine Word is spoken in Jesus' many human words and combines human cognition with God's reason (*ratio Dei*), in which he knows and loves himself in Logos and pneuma.

The gospels were written down in order to bear witness to the truth of the Church's proclamation. However, our encounter with Jesus is not just in the Book of Books; rather, it is a living encounter with him in his word and sacrament. And for that reason all the books that have ever been written about him will never exhaust his mystery (cf. Jn 21:24f.). But they are necessary in order to testify to his truth, "so that you may come to believe that Jesus is the Messiah, the Son of God, and that through believing you may have life in his name" (Jn 20:31).

God's truth is for us inexhaustible. And this applies not only to God's mystery before it was revealed, i.e., as we know God in his eternal power and divinity through the works of his creation, but also in his existence as Creator of the world, without being able to grasp him in his essence. It also applies after God's revelation of himself and this revelation's being fully present in the Word become flesh and in the Holy Spirit; even then we are still unable to grasp God as if he were an object of our natural, empirically bound understanding, that is, so that we could empirically prove or disprove his necessary existence. He remains a mystery, not one clothed in darkness, of course, but one bathed in a superabundance of light. Only through Jesus' humanity and its presence in the Church and the sacraments do we have a share in the truth and life of God in Jesus Christ.

In order for us to be able to make our defense (*apo-logia*) of the Logos, "the hope that is in you" (1 Pt 3:15), we must reflect on our faith. We do not have a positivist understanding of revelation. The word of God was not dictated in Hebrew or Aramaic to an angel in heaven, who then confided it to a chosen prophet to mechanically pass on. God meets us in the life and preaching of the Son of God as the Word that became flesh. If the word of God took on human form in Jesus, its adoption in the faith community of the Church must also have a history, that is, the history leading to the definitive understanding of the dogma. But this is not always a matter of recognizing something new; rather, in the course of the history of the Church and of dogma we acquire, comprehend, and communicate an ever deeper understanding of what is unsupersedably (*un-überbietbar*) new, the *Verbum incarnatum*, in all its richness.

Christ entrusted the witness of his work of salvation to the apostles. And that is why the apostle Paul thanks the Thessalonians that they accepted his human words of preaching not as just a human word about God but as God's word in the human word (cf. 1 Thess 2:13). Belief in the divine intellect, the Logos, is already in itself intellectual. We must on no account reduce it to blind trust. Faith is not just trusting that you are justified through Christ's merits. It cannot be separated from its content as the knowledge and profession that Jesus is the Lord and rose from the dead (cf. Rom 10:9). It is a gamble of self-giving; but it is not a reckless jump over a dark abyss.

THEOLOGY PROMOTES FAITH

Faith is always cognition because it is a sharing in the mutual knowledge of Father and Son in the Holy Spirit. That is why the faith of the Church has rational structures and why its teaching can be communicated as dia-logue because it is in itself dia-logical and thus logical, albeit not one-dimensionally and self-reflectively but rather in a relationally dialogical fashion. When we reject fideism, don't let us go to the opposite extreme of reducing faith rationalistically to the mental capacity of the created intellect or even of making instrumental reason the criterion for what we accept or reject as reasonable and scientifically provable in God's self-revelation in his Logos and pneuma. Faith does not have to justify itself before the tribunal of man's fallible reason but only before that of inerrant divine reason, in which the infallibility of the Church shares in her faith and doctrine.

Truth is reason and reason is truth. All belief in God's truth is participation in God's reason. The *lumen naturale* of human reason transcends itself in the *lumen fidei*, when reason allows itself to be enlightened by the Holy Spirit. The inner unity between faith and reason results in the need for a rational reflection of faith. Faith is neither derived from reason nor reduced to it. But Catholic theology as a function of the Church understands its cognitive principle to be *fides quaerens intellectum* (Anselm of Canterbury).

One could ask why it is not possible to completely grasp the Catholic faith intellectually and conceptually once and for all. Is it not enough if we just produce critical editions of the works of the Church Fathers and keep on reprinting them? Or who would ever want to try to think up something new when St. Thomas Aquinas, that greatest of intellectuals produced by the Catholic Church after St. Augustine, already reached the pinnacle of a synthesis between faith and reason in his *Summa theologiae*? Or who would want to better Newman's theory of the development of doctrine or to say something that is not already to be found in Romano Guardini, Yves Congar, Henri de Lubac, Karl Rahner, Hans Urs von Balthasar, Josef Ratzinger, and many other outstanding contemporary theologians?

It is right that we must always be schooled in the writings of St. Thomas and must not fall behind his level of reflection. But it is equally right and important not just to mechanically repeat the intellectual achievements of our forebears but rather to make them our own and update them creatively in an intellectual process and in dialogue with the contemporary human and natural sciences. Until the end of the world, we shall never succeed in intellectually processing and writing down what Jesus did and what he meant and means for us yesterday, today, and tomorrow, for "the world itself could not contain the books that would be written" (Jn 21:25), which is how John concludes his gospel of the Logos who is God and took on our flesh.

Theology is the science of the *Verbum incarnatum*. There will be no end to studying theological books and to the constant mediation of faith and reason that lies behind them until the Lord appears in glory and we see him face to face in the *lumen gloriae*. Then we shall recognize the complete rationality of revelation as the substance of what we have grasped in faith and embraced in hope when we in our pilgrim state could not yet see the goal of our faith (cf. Heb 11:1). The difference between belief and unbelief will be made manifest to all after death. The faithful will see the One in whom they believed. Unbelievers will see the One in whom they did not believe.

Catholic theology distinguishes itself from every kind of idealist or rationalist metaphysics by its inexhaustible humility. It bows down before the mystery of God, never wishing to reduce it to a single concept, or to force revelation into a regulative idea of reason, or to subject the word of God to a postulate of moral reason, or even to devalue God into a surface on which to project our own religious feelings. Faith rests on God's real and historical self-revelation and has its firm foundation in the Incarnation of the Logos—the Son of the Father—in the salvific events connected with this: his Passion, death, and Resurrection; the sending of the Spirit; and Christ's coming again at the end of history. The priest's mindset, his *forma mentis*, must nowadays be shaped by a synthetic overall picture of the areas where the focus must lie in communicating the faith today. Let us not allow so-called liberalism to dissuade us from dogma as an outdated mode of thinking; for what it means is intellectually sharing in God's self-knowledge in his Logos, who became flesh.

When he was made a cardinal in 1879, John Henry Newman characterized these two attitudes: dogmatic thinking is the recognition of the authority of the self-revealing God, whereas liberalism is subjecting the truths of divine revelation to one's own judgment.

In dogma, the Catholic Church relates faith to facts of salvation history, to the metaphysical principles of the reality of truth and the truth of being, and not to speculative theories and historical constructions. Theology is not a matter of feeling and practical interest. St. Ambrose offers us a guideline for Catholic theologians: "*Non in dialectica complacuit Deo salvum facere populum suum*" (*De fide* I,5)—It is not the will of God to save his people through dialectics and logical sophistry; rather, he wants to give them the security and certainty of assenting reasonably to faith. What determines the content of "theology" comes from reflecting on its necessity as a "function of the Church" (Dietrich Bonhoeffer). The Church's mission to proclaim the gospel to people of all times and highly diverse cultures (cf. Mt 28:19) includes the commission to convey revelation in an appropriate form of language and testimony. Only in this way can people with all their different intellectual, psychological, and sociocultural givens receive the revelation of salvation history in faith and allow it to sustainably shape their lives and focus them on their supernatural destiny in eternal life. For this reason, theology, in its effort to theoretically acquire and practically implement revelation, belongs essentially to the Church's universal magisterium.

So theology does not spring from the hubris of reason, which ventures too far into the divine mystery and, instead of risking the necessary leap of faith, wants to stand still on the safe basis of disposing knowledge (*verfügendes Wissen*). Nor is theology based on the private interests of individual researchers. Theology is a task for the whole Church. Its forum is the general public in intellectual and cultural life.

THEOLOGY IN DIALOGUE
WITH THE SCIENCES

With Vatican II, we can define the aim of a lifelong study of theology in its own disciplines and in conjunction with questions of philosophy and the natural sciences as well as in connection with ecumenical issues and the findings of the history of religion as follows: "that the students will correctly draw out Catholic doctrine from divine revelation, profoundly penetrate it, make it the food of their own spiritual lives, and be enabled to proclaim, explain, and protect it in their priestly ministry" (*OT* 16).

In the Pastoral Constitution "On the Church in the Modern World," Vatican II speaks of the mutual enrichment of Church and world. The world has an interest in the Church's moral and social contribution towards the positive development of mankind. But the Church also owes a lot to the world for carrying out her mission to be, in Christ, the sacrament of salvation for all people. "The experience of past ages, the progress of the sciences, and the treasures hidden in the various forms of human culture, by all of which the nature of man himself is more clearly revealed and new roads to truth are opened, these profit the Church, too" (*GS* 44).

Without an academic and therefore scientific theology, it would be impossible to meet the challenges posed by digitalization, globalization, the technological revolution, and the concomitant mentality change in the younger generation. Theology must pave the way for a new Christian humanism. Responsibility for the modern world and each and everyone's hope in God are what should point the way for theology today.

> Indeed this accommodated preaching of the revealed word ought to remain the law of all evangelization. For thus the ability to express Christ's message in its own way is developed in each nation, and at the same time there is fostered a living exchange between the Church and the diverse cultures of people. To promote such exchange, especially in our days, the Church requires the special help of those who live in the world, are versed in different institutions and specialties, and grasp their innermost significance in the eyes of both believers and unbelievers. With the help of the Holy Spirit, it is the task of the entire People of God, especially pastors and theologians, to hear, distinguish and interpret the many voices of our age, and to judge them in the light of the divine word, so that revealed truth can always be more deeply penetrated, better understood and set forth to greater advantage. (*GS* 44)

Without a profound grasp of theology, a priest cannot fulfill his task today. But theology is merely a tool, not the goal of proclamation and pastoral care. But let us not forget the words of the great theologian and apostle to the nations: "And if I [. . .] understand all mysteries and all knowledge, and if I have all faith, so as to remove mountains, but do not have love, I am nothing" (1 Cor 13:2).

Dear Confreres, Dear Fellow Christians,

It is only through cultivating an intense spiritual life and a serious study of theology that we priests will be able to do justice to the hopes people place in us. In the Decree on Priestly Training the fathers of the Second Vatican Council expressed their conviction, which I share, that: "Animated by the spirit of Christ, this sacred synod is fully aware that the desired renewal of the whole Church depends to a great extent on the ministry of its priests" (*OT* 1).

Let us dedicate our whole lives to this end. And let us remain united in prayer. *Oremus pro invicem.*

NOTES

1. The patrologist Michael Fiedrowicz has kindly produced a German annotated systematic collection of patristic source texts on the theology and spirituality of the priestly office: *Quellentexte zur Theologie und Spiritualität des priesterlichen Amtes* (Fohren-Linden 2013).

2. Jean-Jacques Rousseau, *Contrat social*, 1762.

3. Cf. Immanuel Kant, *Die Religion innerhalb der Grenzen der bloßen Vernunft* (Religion within the Boundaries of Mere Reason), 1794.

4. Gerhard Ludwig Müller, *Katholische Dogmatik. Für Studium und Praxis der Theologie*, Freiburg 2017. The English version, *Catholic Dogmatics for the Study and Practice of Theology*, is being published in separate volumes, only the first of which, covering creation and eschatology, has appeared to date.

5. Cf. Gerhard Ludwig Müller, *Priestertum und Diakonat. Der Empfänger des Weihesakramentes in schöpfungstheologischer und christologischer Perspektive* (the same as Sammlung Horizonte NF 33), Freiburg 2000. This has appeared in English as *Priesthood and Diaconate: The Recipient of the Sacrament of Holy Orders from the Perspective of Creation Theology and Christology*, trans. Michael J. Miller (San Francisco: Ignatius, 2002). Also cf. *Der Empfänger des Weihesakraments. Quellen zur Lehre und Praxis der Kirche, nur Männern das Weihesakrament zu spenden*, Würzburg 1999; *Von "Inter Insigniores" bis "Ordinatio Sacerdotalis." Dokumente und Studien der Glaubenskongregation* (the same as Römische Texte und Studien 3), Würzburg 2006.

6. Georg W. F. Hegel, *Philosophie der Weltgeschichte* I, 63 (PhB 171a).

7. Georg W. F. Hegel, *Philosophie der Weltgeschichte* IV, 822 (PhB 171d).

8. Gotthold Ephraim Lessing, *Über den Beweis des Geistes und der Kraft* (On the Proof of the Spirit and of Power), 1777.

9. Thomas à Kempis, *The Imitation of Christ* IV, 5; cf. *Cat. Rom.* II, 8,22.

10. Cf. Johann Adam Möhler, *Symbolik* §25.

11. Johann Adam Möhler, *Symbolik* §36.

12. David Friedrich Strauss, *Das Leben Jesu, kritisch betrachtet,* Tübingen 1835/36.

13. Cf. Hans Joas, *Die Macht des Heiligen. Eine Alternative zur Geschichte von der Entzauberung,* Berlin 2017, 355ff.

14. Cf. Henri de Lubac, *Le drame de l'humanisme athée* (Paris: Spes, 1944), published in English as *The Drama of Atheist Humanism,* trans. M. Riley, A. Nash, M. Sebanc (San Francisco: Ignatius, 1995—translation of the 1983 edition including chapters omitted from the 1949 translation).

15. The German word *geistlich* can be translated as "spiritual" or "clerical," but also as "religious," "sacred," etc. depending on the context. *Ein Geistlicher* contains and combines all these meanings and is used for a minister of religion, being translated differently according to denomination (transl.).

16. An excellent account of this is offered by Stefan Heid, *Zölibat in der frühen Kirche. Die Anfänge der Enthaltsamkeitspflicht für Kleriker in Ost und West,* Paderborn 1997. English translation: *Celibacy in the Early Church: The Beginnings of a Discipline of Obligatory Continence for Clerics in East and West,* trans. Michael J. Miller (San Francisco: Ignatius, 2000).

17. Friedrich Wilhelm Nietzsche, *Jenseits von Gut und Böse.* Vorrede 1 (the same as KSA 5), 11. Engl. transl. *Beyond Good and Evil.* Preface.

Cardinal Gerhard Ludwig Müller served as prefect of the Congregation for the Doctrine of the Faith from 2012 to 2017. He was appointed bishop of Regensburg, Germany, in 2002 by Pope John Paul II. Müller was elevated to archbishop in 2012 by Pope Benedict XVI and to cardinal in 2014 by Pope Francis.

Prior to being named prefect, Müller served on the Pontifical Council for Culture, Congregation for Catholic Education, and the Pontifical Council for Promoting Christian Unity. After Müller's appointment as archbishop and prefect, he also became *ex officio* president of the Pontifical Biblical Commission, the International Theological Commission, and the Pontifical Commission *Ecclesia Dei*.

Müller retired in 2017. He has written more than six hundred works on various topics including dogmatic theology, revelation, ecumenism, and the diaconate. He is the editor of the *Complete Works of Joseph Ratzinger—Pope Benedict XVI* in sixteen volumes.